BEYOND THE SPECTACLE
OF TERRORISM

◆

THE RADICAL IMAGINATION SERIES
Edited by Henry A. Giroux and Stanley Aronowitz

Now Available

Beyond the Spectacle of Terrorism: Global Uncertainty and the Challenge of the New Media
   by Henry A. Giroux

Forthcoming

A Future for the American Left
   by Stanley Aronowitz

Afromodernity: How Europe Is Evolving toward Africa
   by Jean Comaroff and John L. Comaroff

BEYOND THE SPECTACLE OF TERRORISM
Global Uncertainty and the Challenge of the New Media

HENRY A. GIROUX

Paradigm Publishers

Boulder • London

Copyright © 2006 by Paradigm Publishers

Published in the United States by Paradigm Publishers, 3360 Mitchell Lane Suite E, Boulder, Colorado 80301 USA.

Paradigm Publishers is the trade name of Birkenkamp & Company, LLC, Dean Birkenkamp, President and Publisher.

Library of Congress Cataloging-in-Publication Data

Giroux, Henry A.
    Beyond the spectacle of terrorism : global uncertainty and the challenge of the new media / Henry A. Giroux.
        p. cm. — (Radical imagination)
    Includes bibliographical references and index.
    ISBN 1-59451-239-6 (hc) — ISBN 1-59451-240-X (pbk) 1. Terrorism. 2. Democracy. 3. Internet. 4. Reality television programs. I. Title. II.
Series.
    HV6431.G547 2006
    303.6'25—dc22

                                                          2005033050

Printed and bound in the United States of America on acid-free paper that meets the standards of the American National Standard for Permanence of Paper for Printed Library Materials.

Designed and Typeset by Straight Creek Bookmakers.

10   09   08   07   06
1   2   3   4   5

To Susan, who has given me a life I would never have imagined.

Contents

Acknowledgments   ix

Acts of Translation: The Crisis of Democracy in
the Age of Fear — An Introduction   1

Rethinking the Politics of the Spectacle in the
Society of the Image   19

Index   97

About the Author   105

◇

Acknowledgments

I want to thank Susan Searls Giroux, John Comaroff, Roger Simon, Arif Dirlik, David Theo Goldberg, Stanley Aronowitz, Lawrence Grossberg, and Nick Couldry for providing me with a number of critical insights and suggestions that otherwise would not have been in this paper. While I am solely responsible for the paper, their critical input was invaluable in helping me think through the various ideas I take up in this piece. I also want to thank Nasrin Rahimieh, Ken Saltman, and Max Haiven for their critical input. I am deeply indebted to my graduate assistant, Grace Pollock, who brought all of her creative and critical editorial skills to bear on this manuscript, and, as a consequence, it is much better because of her professional help. My administrative assistant, Maya Stamenkovic, could not have done a better job in creating an atmosphere conducive to my work. Donaldo Macedo, my brother, has always been there for me and even more so as I was writing this book.

As usual, Dean Birkenkamp, my friend and publisher, has provided invaluable support and insight in bringing this book to press. It is an amazing experience to have a publisher who is as brilliant as he is professional. I feel blessed having him in my life, as I know do many of his other authors.

In choosing an image for the cover of this book, I wanted to use a representation that was not news-specific, one whose representational politics captured less the singularity of a particular spectacular event, expression of suffering, or form of abuse than an image that signified a more general, ambiguous representation of both the spectacle of terrorism and the barbarism it evokes. I decided right off not to use an image with a literalness that might be exploitative—photos of the Twin Towers burning, individuals wounded and bleeding, or context-specific acts of barbarism such as someone about to be beheaded. Hence, I did not want to use either historically specific images, such as those that would be unmistakably associated with Abu Ghraib, Iraq, Palestine, Israel, or Chechnya, or those directly related to the events of 9/11. Instead, I chose this non-news-specific image precisely because of its ambiguity. In an age when the appeal to terrorism—the spectacle of terrorism, to be more exact—is used by state and nonstate terrorists alike to appropriate fear as a pretext for the most horrendous crimes, I think the image I've selected reminds us not of the singularity of the particular person behind the hood (is it a woman, a victim of CIA counter-terrorism, a journalist captured by extremist groups in Iraq who is about to be beheaded?) but of the larger political forces that create such horrors through conditions that make such horrendous images and crimes even possible. The cover illustrates an ambivalence about the image that ranges from diplomats who have been kidnapped, Iraqis who have been tortured, dissidents who have been abducted, black men who have been abused in U.S. prisons, students who have been tortured by the police in any one of a number of oppressive regimes—and it invites the most awful play of imagination suggesting that the image could be me, you, any of us, and that our lives are not so removed from the play of these forces as to allow us to be either complacent about such acts or, even worse, morally and politically indifferent. And even if the image cannot be imagined privately, it evokes the question of what our responsibility might be to this person behind the hood, not merely/only/exclusively as an ethical question (which is impossible) but also as an educational and political issue. What kind of responsibility do we have to the man, woman, or child who is masked? The image graphically evokes not simply our own vulnerability but also, along with the title's call to move "beyond," our complicity. After all, that image is everywhere and it indicts us all. What I like about the ambiguity of the image is that it does not register one specific historical moment such as Abu Ghraib. It is decontextualized in the same way the figure is: This could be anyone, including one of us, and thus says something about both our vulnerability and, more important, our responsibility to address the conditions that create not just the image but the suffering it suggests—a form of suffering that take place within particular forms of material and symbolic relations of power.

◇

Acts of Translation

The Crisis of Democracy in the Age of Fear — An Introduction

Democracy begins to fail and political life becomes impoverished when society can no longer translate private problems into social issues. Unfortunately, that is precisely what is happening in the United States today. In the post-9/11 world, the space of shared responsibility has given way to the space of private fears; the social obligations of citizenship are now reduced to the highly individualized imperatives of consumerism, and militarism has become a central motif of national identity. In this cold new world, the language of politics is increasingly mediated through a spectacle of terrorism in which fear and violence become central modalities through which to grasp the meaning of self in society. While efforts to collapse the public into the private have a long history in American political culture, such attempts have taken on a new forcefulness in the age of terror as nation-states have become both more authoritarian and increasingly vulnerable to assault from unknown sources. Law and violence have become indistinguishable as societies enter into a legitimation crisis, unable to guarantee protection to their citizens while intensifying a culture of fear that appears to mimic the very practices

1

used by nonstate terrorists to spread their ideologies.[1] As the war on terrorism takes aim at justice, democracy, and political autonomy, images of hatred, violence, and destruction become enshrined in the special effects made possible by new media technologies such as camcorders, mobile camera-phones, satellite television, digital recorders, and the Internet. Screen culture has emerged as a crucial pedagogical tool, administering a 24–hour series of visceral shocks to viewers, radically displacing their former selves as consumers of material goods; now they are organized largely through shared fears rather than shared responsibilities. Under the spectacle of terrorism, the state relies more heavily on its security functions, and nonstate terrorists rewrite the space of the political and social through a circuit of anxiety, panic, destruction, and revenge that makes an ethical response moot and a democratic conception of politics, in the words of Attorney General Alberto Gonzales, "quaint." As the culture of fear and the spectacle of terrorism become indistinguishable, everyday life undergoes a structural and political transformation, fusing sophisticated, electronic technologies with a ubiquitous screen culture while simultaneously expanding the range of cultural producers and recipients of information and images.[2]

As the public collapses into the personal, the personal becomes "the only politics there is, the only politics with a tangible referent or emotional valence."[3] Within the pervasive discourse of neoliberalism, the citizen has been reduced to a consumer, and needs have become utterly privatized. It is by such an utterly personal discourse that human actions are shaped and agency is increasingly marshaled within an image-based culture that mobilizes fear, insecurity, and resentment in order to reassert personal safety and homeland security as the most important dimensions of political culture and life. Just as violence is staged as a global spectacle, language, sound, and image lose their critical functions as they are turned into weapons to combat an enemy that is ubiquitous and to glorify a politics mobilized around an unrelenting campaign of fear. Under such circumstances, the language of the social is devalued as the call for state protection translates into the suspension of civil liberties, new and expanding networks of government surveillance, and the increasingly accepted view that dissent is un-American and aids terrorism. The very concept of the public has been thoroughly debased; now it is often equated with a zone of pathology, resulting in its privatization and militarization. For instance, in contemporary political discourse, "public schools," "public transportation," and "public welfare" have become dirty words—code for sites of contamination, disorder, and violence. Where the public is not seen as a site of disorder, it is sold off to private interests. All dreams of the future are now modeled around the narcissistic, privatized, and self-indulgent needs of consumer culture and increasingly honed to respond to new markets produced by the omniscient culture of fear. Stripped of its ethical and political importance, the public interest has been largely fashioned as a giant Reality TV show where notions of collectivity register as a conglomeration of private concerns—possessive individualism, the cult of celebrity, and unbridled competition—resulting in communities with nothing in common save for a nagging sense of impending danger. As globalization breaks down barriers to trade, information, and capital—but also surveillance and terrorism—the public feels more vulnerable as it is overwhelmed by forces that it neither understands nor believes are under its control.[4] Such insecurities are fed by the hollowing out of the state, which no longer seems capable of supporting the notion of a social contract, guaranteeing a secure future, and investing government resources in the public good or even using such resources to address major disasters and everyday social problems, as Hurricane Katrina made clear. Now Reality TV comes to the fore as a way of both making the world more intelligible and legitimating a world in which self-reliance, rabid competition, and a kind of pathological individualism become the norm. Within such circumstances, as Grace Pollock points out, Reality TV "provides a consumable fantasy in which people's fears and uncertainties are subdued by the pursuit of private pleasure, particularly through identification with the structure of Reality TV shows—especially interactive ones that empower the audience to vote and actually participate in inflicting pain on others—and snuff films that reduce human relations to a physical battle between the all-powerful and the utterly powerless."[5]

As the very idea of the social collapses into the private realm of the self and its fears, it becomes more difficult for people to develop a vocabulary for understanding how individual insecurity, dread, and misery could be translated into concerns of an engaged and critical citizenry. Instead, they are told that their privately held misery is a fall from grace, a flaw in character that must be suffered in isolation. Poverty, for example, is now imagined to be a problem of individual failing. Racism is rationalized and represented as simply an act of individual discrimination or prejudice. Homelessness is reduced to a freely chosen decision made by lazy people. Misfortune is a private disgrace or deserving of only a sneer. Most important, fear and anxiety do not translate into a vigilant concern about the existing status of democracy or the public good but are reduced to heightened demands for protection from others.

Democracy relies on a kind of political imagination and collective hope that allows us to move from the personal to the political and back again. It revolves, as Alain Badiou argues, around the willingness of those who believe in a democracy to show "how the space of the possible is larger than the one assigned—that something else is possible, but not everything is possible."[6] Translating the private into the public, then, is about more than enlarging the realm of critique and affirming the existence of the common good; it is also about public responsibility, the struggle over democratic public life, and the importance of rethinking, in particular, how an image-based culture and new electronic technologies are shaping the direction of public pedagogy and political culture in an increasingly fragile democratic society.

Any viable politics of hope and meaning must address how each of our lives is related to the greater common good and what it means to create the conditions for seeing ourselves as citizens who govern as well as those who are governed. If, in the age of terrorism, we lack the language, desire, and visions for raising questions about who we are as a society and what we want our society as a whole to accomplish, then we run the risk of compromising any vestige of democracy as part of our lived politics. In short, we lack what philosopher Zygmunt Bauman has argued makes a democratic politics viable at all.[7] This collective failure of vision, imagination, ethical responsibility, and direction has led to a growing authoritarianism that encourages profit-driven mega-monopolies, the seductions of faith-based certainty, the militarization of everyday life, and the undermining of any vestige of critical education, responsible dissent, and public dialogue. Mass uncertainty accompanies the endless bad news about neoliberal capitalism with its downsizing and contract labor policies, its gutting of social provisions, and its contempt for the public good. Economic insecurity coupled with the fear of random violence now provides the conditions for more prisons, besieged cities, gated communities, galloping intrusions on privacy, increased surveillance, and the emergence of a police state. Increasingly unable to grasp how questions of power, politics, history, and public consciousness interface with new media that collapse a culture of terror into private fears and uncertainties, many people either refuse or find it difficult to reactivate their political sensibilities and conceive of themselves as engaged social agents. Social agency, if not democratic politics itself, appears to be in decline as the conviction that "society can be changed for the better ... has greatly diminished."[8] The impoverishment of public life enables the ascent of authoritarianism just as it undercuts the possibility of dissent and the political imagination itself. Defense Secretary Donald Rumsfeld's claim that "the war will be won when Americans and their children will again be able to 'feel safe'" increasingly prompts us to ask whether the war he is referencing is one being waged not against terrorists but against democratic freedoms,[9] especially at a time when war has become the foundation for all social practices and relations of power.

One of the more significant characteristics of an authoritarian society is its willingness to trade in the rhetoric of fear in order to manipulate the public into a state of servile, apolitical dependency and unquestioning ideological support. The American public is inundated and partly enamored by images of fear, violence, and policing, highlighted in endless television police dramas, newspaper articles, popular magazines, and Reality TV programs. The culture of fear and its attendant mediated representations of violence, risk, and policing serve both "as a lightning rod for an escalating range of everyday anxieties"[10] and as a rhetorical umbrella under which to promote other public agendas of aggression and violence. At the same time, the theatricality of modern power, violence, lawlessness, and terrorism is used by the government to produce a sense of helplessness and cynicism throughout the body politic.

Dwight Macdonald, writing in the aftermath of World War II and the horrors of the Nazi Holocaust, situates the rise of authoritarianism in a broader context. He argues that as more and more people are excluded from the experience of political agency and exhibit "less and less control over the 'policies' of their governments," ethics is reduced to the status of mere platitudes, and politics becomes banal.[11] According to Macdonald, as the state becomes more tightly controlled, organized, and rationalized, it empties politics and morality of any substance and relevance, thus making it difficult for people to care about the obligations of critical citizenship or to participate in the broader landscape of politics and power. Under such circumstances, linguistic abstraction and visual symbolism become the mechanisms of choice for promoting political powerlessness as the state misrepresents the truth or trivializes it. The upshot is a public dialogue reduced to mere platitudes reinforcing moral indifference and political impotence—coupled with an arsenal of visual imagery to both excite and incite "shock and awe." In the current political landscape, the truth is not merely misrepresented through language; it is also mediated through image-based media and a visualizing culture that empties meaning of substance, delivering a new kind of spectacle in which the visual is bound to a brutalizing politics of fear and hyped-up forms of terrorist threats.

Under the Bush administration, especially since the horrible events of September 11th, we have witnessed an extension of the concept of war, not only applied to traditional, strategic, defense-oriented objectives, but also used to discipline civil society, reproduce all aspects of public life in the image of official power, and establish the ideologies of militarism and market fundamentalism as the foundation for effective governance. War, fear, and insecurity have become the most powerful principles through which society is organized. Defined as the foundation of politics, war is now invoked as a form of biopolitics and deployed to "criminalize all forms of social contestation and resistance" and legitimate the ongoing "passage from the welfare state to the warfare state."[12] Increasingly accompanying this form of discursive, symbolic, and material repression is the refashioning of language, sound, and image in an effort to diminish the capacity of the American public to weigh evidence critically, exercise thoughtful discrimination, and make informed judgments. As the power of critical understanding is traded for the simulacra of communication in official discourse, it becomes more difficult for citizens to engage in critical debates, translate private considerations into public concerns, and recognize the distortions and omissions that underlie much of the current government policies justified as part of the "war on terrorism."

As U.S. military action spreads abroad under the guise of a permanent war on terrorism, public spaces on the domestic front are increasingly being organized around a highly militarized, patriarchal, and jingoistic set of values that has undermined "centuries of demo-cratic gains."[13] Americans are not only obsessed with military power: "[I]t has become central to our national identity."[14] Andrew J. Bacevich develops this position by arguing that Americans have been seduced by a danger-ous form of militarism. He writes:

> To state the matter bluntly, Americans in our own time have fallen prey to militarism, manifesting it-self in a romanticized view of soldiers, a tendency to see military power as the truest measure of national greatness, and outsized expectations regarding the efficacy of force. To a degree without precedent in U.S. history, Americans have come to define the nation's strength and well-being in terms of military preparedness, military action, and the fostering of (or nostalgia for) military ideals.[15]

How else to explain the fact that the United States has "725 official military bases outside the country and 969 at home"? Or that it "spends more on 'defense' than all the rest of the world put together ... [or that] this country is obsessed with war: rumors of war, im-ages of war, 'preemptive' war, 'preventive' war, 'surgical' war, 'prophylactic' war, 'permanent' war? As President Bush explained at a news conference in April 2004, 'This country must go on the offense and stay on the offense.'"[16] Of course, the process of militarization—the increasing centrality of the military in shaping American culture, society, and foreign policy—has a long history in the United States and takes on different forms under different historical conditions.[17] Unlike the old style of militarization in which all forms of civil authority were subordinate to military authority, the new ethos of militarization is organized as a form of biopolitics designed to engulf the entire social order, legitimating its values as a foundational aspect of American public life. According to journalist George Monbiot, the federal government "is now spending as much on war as it is on education, public health, housing, employment, pensions, food aid and welfare put together."[18] Moreover, the United States is being radically transformed into a national security state, increasingly put under the sway of the military-corporate-industrial-educational complex. The values of the security state, along with its increasing emphasis on militarized surveillance, control, and containment, are gradually permeating our public schools, universities, streets, popular culture, and criminal justice system, aided in great part by the new media with their investment in spectacularizing violence and fear. For example, some universities are establishing formal relations with the FBI in what can only be viewed as another illustration of the emerging power of the national security state. More specifically, under the auspices of the newly established National Security Higher Education Advisory Board, Penn State University, Johns Hopkins University, the University of California at Los Angeles, the University of Pennsylvania, Carnegie Mellon University, and a number of other prominent institutions of higher education have joined with the FBI in order to "establish lines of communication on national priorities pertaining to terrorism, counterintelligence and homeland security. [The Advisory Board] also will assist in the development of research, degree programs, course work, internships, opportunities for graduates and consulting opportunities for faculty related to national security."[19] Leading the Advisory Board is

Penn State President Graham Spanier, who, without the slightest trace of irony, has stated that the new board "sends a positive message that leaders in higher education are willing to assist our nation during these challenging times."[20] One wonders what type of assistance Spanier will provide with regard to those dissident academics protesting the Bush administration's shameful war in Iraq, the escalating violation of civil liberties by the FBI, or the increasingly problematic ties between higher education and the military establishment.

As the culture of fear expands with the new media's strategic use of sophisticated technologies, aggression and "unspeakably transgressive violence"[21] become the driving forces behind a new kind of politics and pedagogy used by both state and corporate power, on the one hand, and stateless insurgents, on the other. Memory and fantasy entwine as actual and imaginary events fuse in a orgy of hyper-real violence that conjoins the visceral experience of pain, torture, abuse, and suffering with the spectacular politics of fear. Public space is now saturated with a new order of spectacle that trades in violence in order to either shock or create a desire for, if not a fascination and identification with, practices that reproduce fear and terror in others and in oneself.

As critical thought is attacked and the conditions for its production disabled, the spectacle of terrorism with its appeal to fear, violence, and rabid forms of masculinity mobilizes an aesthetic taste for the combination of high drama and real-life violence and horror. Political theater is now mediated through the elemental—even sacred—forces of sacrifice, redemption, and the triumph of power. The culture of fear combined with the spectacle of terrorism substitutes a sense of compassion and caring for the other with a concern for one's personal security and a deep distrust of others, especially if those others are Arab or Muslim.

This book is an attempt to examine the centrality of the new media not only as a political and pedagogical force that has become a defining feature of the culture of fear—invoked by state and nonstate groups alike—but also as a new technology for redefining the very nature of politics itself. Unlike traditional theories of the spectacle and the aestheticization of politics, especially fascist aestheticization and the spectacle of consumerism, my argument is that the new media provide the conditions, within the existing global war on terrorism and culture of fear, for an extension of the logic of militarism to the realm of the symbolic and that the central elements of the spectacle of terrorism are unlike anything we have seen in the past—given their enshrinement of hyper-real violence, their unadulterated appeal to fear, their diverse forms of resistance to state power, and their elevation of the image to a prominent feature of social and political power. The emergence of the spectacle of terrorism as a new form of public pedagogy raises serious questions about how fear and anxiety can be marketed, how terrorism can be used to recruit people in support of authoritarian causes, how it is being produced in a vast array of pedagogical sites created by the new media, how the state uses mediated images of violence to justify its monopoly of power over the means of coercion, and how the spectacle of terrorism works in an age of enormous injustices, deep insecurities, disembodied social relations, fragmented communities, and a growing militarization of everyday life. At the same time, there is the crucial question of how the new media can be used to expand rather than close down democratic relations. What agents, conditions, contents, and structural transformations are necessary to rethink the centrality of the new media within an advanced society so as to configure social practices within rather than outside of the realm of democratic values, identities, and social relations?

While much has been written about the state of emergency as a construct for engaging the growing authoritarianism of contemporary American society waged under the banner of the war on terrorism, I want to theorize the relationship between terrorism and the development of the security state through the concept of the spectacle so as to highlight in new and significant ways not only the educational force of the culture—what I call public pedagogy—but also the importance of the new media, with their electronic technologies and image-based production. At stake here is the notion that the culture of fear, the discourse of terrorism, and the social relations forged by these forces cannot be understood outside of how the spectacle of terrorism undermines and limits democracy. A spreading orgy of global violence now links the power of the image with the culture of fear and has opened up a new space for understanding the political as a pedagogical force and the spectacle as the means of politics. The tangible effects of violence are now made visible through the theatrical staging efforts of both state and nonstate terrorists. "Shock and awe" videos are aired on the nightly news right alongside beheading videos (though the actual act is never shown on mainstream media outlets). War, violence, and politics have taken on a new disturbing form and sense of urgency within image-based cultures—and, as politics increasingly is constituted outside of the law, one of its first victims is democracy itself.

As the spectacle of terrorism becomes a major organizing principle of all aspects of daily life, it is all the more imperative for educators, artists, parents, students, and others to develop a language of critique and possibility capable of expressing what is new and different in the constantly shifting interface of politics and culture today. In part, this means overcoming the despair, cynicism, and economic reductionism that characterize so much of left-oriented theory while simultaneously challenging the accommodating logic of a toothless liberalism and the increasing barbarism of unaccountable power embraced by right-wing conservatives. Questions regarding the interface of politics, pedagogy, and culture must be addressed as part of the challenge to connect matters of power, ideology, and resistance with a conception of individual and social agency informed by the promise of a radical democracy. Struggles over culture must be viewed as crucial to struggles over meaning and identity, and must be understood within broader structural and discursive relations of power, especially those supporting new communication-based technologies such as the Internet. The immensely productive nature of violence, both as spectacle and as policy, must be addressed within a politics of culture attentive to the material relations that underlie its effectiveness. Culture is the site where a radical politics can emerge that takes seriously the everyday experiences through which people give meaning to their lives, particularly in the intersections of actual, lived experiences and the representations through which those experiences are mediated and shaped.

The politics of culture and the culture of politics need to be addressed within a new radical imaginary and biopolitics in order to analyze not only how the new media function as a sophisticated tool for pacification and depoliticization but also how their technologies, power, and global reach provide a means for new and emancipatory modes of communication, exchange, and intervention in the world. As a result of the emergence of new technologies of diffusion, culture becomes more globalized as it is newly hybridized and organized through technologies that redefine its meaning, the power of its reach, and the influence it has in shaping diverse and loosely connected audiences. Produced, organized, and circulated within global circuits of power, culture can no longer be reduced to an instrument of market culture; it also has become a powerful force for the reproduction of public spheres engaged in the production of a global landscape of violence, fear, and insecurity. But the globalization of culture is more than a dystopian narrative in which culture is exclusively equated with market relations and sutured forms of domination. It is also a complex, shifting, and often contradictory space in which conditions emerge for developing new critical tools, counter-public spheres, modes of resistance, social movements, and institutions dedicated to the creation of democratic global public spheres. This suggests rethinking how regimes of representation might work to make democratic politics visible, undermine the primacy of violence as a legitimating tool, provide a space for personal and collective memory-work, and reimagine the role of the state outside of its narrow appeal to policing functions and its drive for capital accumulation.

In what follows, I argue that the spectacle of terrorism has to be comprehended and critically engaged if we are to prevent the present age from sliding into a wild zone of violence and lawlessness. Understanding the new media and the role they play in the production of a culture of fear and politics of authoritarianism is one of the great challenges faced by anyone and everyone concerned about the future of democracy. While neither the pursuit of democracy nor the overcoming of violence is about simply the production and circulation of images, the struggle for global democracy must develop a politics in which the connection between the symbolic and material relations of power is theorized in ways that are thoroughly appropriate to the particularities of place and the historical crisis in which we now find ourselves. But as crucial as this task is, it is not enough. The search for new theories about the political and pedagogical roles played by the spectacle of terrorism in an image-based society must also include a politics of hope. In this instance, the new media can be critically engaged in terms of their radical possibilities as part of a cultural politics and public pedagogy that allow for a more imaginative and rigorous grasp of the promise of a democratic future organized through a plurality of democratic discourses, values, identities, and public spheres.[22]

Notes

1. This issue is brilliantly analyzed by Jean and John Comaroff in "Criminal Obsessions, After Foucault: Postcoloniality, Policing, and the Metaphysics of Disorder," *Critical Inquiry* 30 (Summer 2004): 800–824.

2. For a definitive analysis of the relationship between the new media and aesthetics, see Lev Manovich, *The Language of the New Media* (Cambridge, MA: MIT Press, 2001).

3. Jean Comaroff and John L. Comaroff, "Millennial Capitalism: First Thoughts on a Second Coming," *Public Culture* 12, no. 2 (Duke University Press, 2000): 305–306.

4. Zygmunt Bauman, "Terrors of the Global," unpublished paper (2005), p. 1.

5. I want to thank Grace Pollock, my graduate assistant, for this insight—conveyed in a private e-mail correspondence dated September 15, 2005.

6. Alain Badiou, *Ethics: An Essay on the Understanding of Evil* (London: Verso, 1998), pp. 115–116.

7. Zygmunt Bauman, "Introduction," *Society Under Siege* (Malden, MA: Blackwell, 2002), p. 170.

8. Stanley Aronowitz and Peter Bratsis, "Situations Manifesto," *Situations* 1, no.1 (April 2005): 7.

9. Rumsfeld cited in William Pfaff, "Still Waiting for a Clear Statement of Attainable War Goals," *International Herald Tribune,* September 27, 2001, available online at http://www.commondreams.org/views01/0927–02.htm.

10. Comaroff and Comaroff, "Criminal Obsessions," p. 804.

11. Dwight Macdonald, *The Responsibility of Intellectuals and Other Essays in Political Criticism* (London: Victor Gollancz, 1957), pp. 44–45.

12. Michael Hardt and Antonio Negri, *Multitude: War and Democracy in the Age of Empire* (New York: Penguin Press, 2004), pp. 15–16.

13. Susan Buck-Morss, *Thinking Past Terror: Islamism and Critical Theory on the Left* (New York/London: Verso, 2003), p. 33.

14. Andrew J. Bacevich, *The New American Militarism* (New York: Oxford University Press, 2005), p. 1.

15. Ibid., p. 2.

16. Tony Judt, "The New World Order," *New York Review of Books* 52:12 (July 14, 2005): 16.

17. John R. Gillis, ed., *The Militarization of the Western World* (New Brunswick: Rutgers University Press, 1989). On the militarization of urban space, see Mike Davis, *City of Quartz* (New York: Vintage, 1992), and Kenneth Saltman and David Gabbard, eds., *Education as Enforcement: The Militarization and Corporatization of Schools* (New York: Routledge, 2003). For an analysis of the current neoconservative influence on militarizing American foreign policy, see Donald Kagan and Gary Schmidt, *Rebuilding America's Defenses* (2000), which was developed under the auspices of The Project for the New American Century (http://www.newamericancentury.org). It is one of many reports outlining this issue.

18. George Monbiot, "States of War," *The Guardian/UK*, October 14, 2003, available online at http://www.commondreams.org/views03/1014–09.htm.

19. Penn State News Release, "Penn State's Spanier to Chair National Security Board" (Friday, September 16, 2005).

20. Marissa Carl, "Spanier to Head New FBI Board," *The Digital Collegian* (Monday, September 19, 2005), available online at http://www.collegian.psu.edu/archive/2005/09/09–19–05tdc/09-19-05dnews-05.asp.

21. Comaroff and Comaroff, "Criminal Obsessions," p. 807.

22. I am taking this idea from Stanley Aronowitz, "Commentary," in Mark Poster, *The Information Subject* (Amsterdam: Gordon and Breach, 2001), pp. 177–178.

◊

Rethinking the Politics of the Spectacle in the Society of the Image

The whole situation changes as soon as all available modern means [of war] are allied to the highly symbolic weapon of their own death. It multiplies the destructive potential ad infinitum. This multiplication of factors (which to us seem irreconcilable) gives the terrorists such superiority. The zero death strategy of a "clean" technological war misses the point of this transfiguration of "real" power by symbolic power.

—*Jean Baudrillard*[1]

The war on terror is a war of images, the firepower of the world's television cameras striking an asymmetric balance against the weapons of mass destruction in the Pentagon's arsenal of fear.

—*Lewis H. Lapham*[2]

It is impossible to comprehend the political nature of the existing age without recognizing the centrality of the new visual media.[3] No longer peripheral to public life, these new media—camcorders, cellular camera-phones, satellite television, digital recorders, the Internet—have enacted a structural transformation of everyday life by fusing sophisticated electronic technologies with a ubiquitous screen culture while simultaneously changing the cultural production and consumption of information and images.[4] Enabling modes of spectatorship that cannot be collapsed into a monolithic mass, they deploy unheard-of powers in the shaping of time, space, knowledge, values, identities, and social relations. Not only have these new mass and image-based media, with their new digital and electronic technologies, revolutionized the relationship between the specificity of an event and its public display by making events accessible to a global audience; they have also ushered in a new regime of the spectacle in which screen culture and visual politics create spectacular events just as much as they record them.[5] Given that screen culture now dominates much of everyday life in the developed countries, the "audio-visual mode has become our primary way of coming in contact with the world and at the same time being detached (safe) from it."[6]

In this age of screen culture, audio-visual representations have transformed not only the landscape of production and reception but the very nature of politics itself, particularly the relationships among nationalism, spectacular violence, and new global politics. The new media often combine notions of violence and vulnerability, fear, and uncertainty, with modern communication technologies that are changing the character and function of representations, the way everyday life is experienced, and even the conditions of politics itself. As the relationship between violence and politics is blurred in an era of permanent war, the significance as well as impact of its effects on both a small and large scale are increasingly defined and mediated through the various regimes of representation (defining good and evil, civilization and barbarism, etc.) and fields of vision deployed by the new media.

As the link between the media and power becomes more integrated, the visual theater of terrorism mimics in aesthetic terms the politics of the "official" war on terrorism. Just as the necessity of fighting terror has become the central rationale for war used by the Bush administration and other governments, a visual culture of shock and awe has emerged, made ubiquitous by the Internet and 24–hour cable news shows devoted to representations of the horrific violence associated with terrorism, ranging from aestheticized images of nighttime bombing raids on Iraqi cities to the countervailing imagery of grotesque killings of hostages by Iraqi fundamentalists. The visual theater of terrorism aestheticizes politics as it celebrates a narrow and dogmatic sacralization of politics as war.[7] Raw violence becomes stylized as it is integrated into audio-visual spectacles that shock and massage the mind and emotions with images, meanings, and sounds that heighten an aesthetic of fear and offer the redemptive promise of a world without enemies or infidels. Defined no longer simply as a weapon of war, lawlessness, or a crime against humanity, violence in the "war on terror" has been merged into a media and religious spectacle, signifying a disturbing transformation of contemporary politics.

Echoing the discourse of the "official" war on terrorism, the violence of extremist groups as well as state-sanctioned and corporate violence are understood almost exclusively within the discourse of moral absolutes pitting good against evil. Whether it is President

George W. Bush's claim that "You are either with us or against us"[8] or Osama bin Laden's injunction that "You are either a believer or an infidel,"[9] these repressive binary logics represent a public pedagogy forged in what I call the spectacle of terrorism, which devalues democratic, reasoned debate in favor of feeding an apocalyptic desire for destruction and death. As both an act of cultural production and a consuming practice, the spectacle of terrorism foregrounds a disturbing transformation in the meaning of a politics whose legitimating power is increasingly defined less through the promotion of affordable pleasures associated with consumer culture than through a steady regimen and theatricality of power that endlessly display representations of fear, violence, and vengeance. Fantasy, force, melodrama, and performance now combine to manufacture a notion of politics evoked through displays of violence and threats of terrorism offered up daily by the electronic and print media. If the media are to be believed, every aspect of life, as Brian Massumi has argued, increasingly appears as "a workstation in the mass production line of fear."[10] The loss of privilege, status, and jobs, and the deep-seated sense of uncertainty that shapes neoliberal capitalism are now conjoined and amplified by gathering anxiety, a sense of helplessness, and the dread of random violence. Cities degenerate into besieged fortresses; people of color live with the ongoing fear of incarceration; public schools are transformed into laboratories for police surveillance modeled after prisons; and the general public's understandable desire for security, fanned by an endless array of media-induced panics over the phantom threat of terrorism, becomes fodder for reactionary policies and violent acts by both state and nonstate terrorists alike, all aimed at drawing limits on or rolling back hard-won democratic freedoms. Violence as theater emerges as part of a regime of representation used by the state in order to legitimize its increasingly bold display of force and the militarization of everyday life as its primary function. At the same time, crime and terror merge as violence becomes the only viable mediator of politics, the only form of agency available in a global world where the spaces of lawlessness grow exponentially.[11] The demon of economic uncertainty now combines with the demon of spectacularized violence to make generalized fear a paralyzing condition, rather than an aberration, of everyday life. Located within a "ghost sociability" of the West in which most people do not have to leave home in order to participate in society's rituals and civic culture, the spectacle of terrorism and its hyper-accelerated media technologies now connect people to global society while reinforcing the empty space at the heart of the neoliberal social order.[12] The emergence of the spectacle of terrorism is all the more significant since, as novelist and cultural critic Marina Warner puts it, "in the realm of culture, the character of our representations matter most urgently.... The images we circulate have the power to lead events, not only [to] report them, [and] the new technical media have altered experience and become interwoven with consciousness itself."[13]

Neither the concept of the spectacle nor the practice of terrorism itself is new, each offering a distinct and complex genealogy that has been engaged by a number of contemporary theorists. But the merging of the spectacle, terrorism, war, and politics beginning with the September 11th terrorists attacks on the World

Trade Center in New York City suggests something unique about the deadly power and battle of images in contemporary global culture. A cinematic politics of the visceral has replaced a more measured and thoughtful commentary on human suffering and alienation, the bequeath of a stunned and stunted postwar generation of intellectuals, artists, and others working in the public interest. Representations of fear, panic, vulnerability, and pain increasingly override narratives of social justice; pure entertainment, as a return to the hyper-real, enshrines audio-visual representations of the gruesome, opening up a new and "important chapter ... in the contemporary war of images."[14] Death and suffering are now inscribed in the order of politics and the power of the image such that the alliance between terror and security in the contemporary era cannot be understood outside of how the spectacle shapes and legitimates social relations. This new chapter in the politics of media no longer simply turns individuals into shoppers or reproduces the logic of commodification; on the contrary, the ingestion of market-driven fantasies has given way to a consumption of fear, dread, and degradation. Powerful images now register a kind of premodern violence as part of a broader strategy of shock that is meant to either paralyze people with fear or justify their indulgence in grotesque fantasies, allegedly sanctioned by the divine, which allow them to watch the ritualistic degradation of other human beings. Or, when the spectacle of terrorism is used by governments, as in President George W. Bush's celebration of "shock and awe" as a form of spectacularized violence, it becomes the primary pedagogical tool to incorporate the populace into the racial fantasies of empire and the illusion of national triumphalism packaged as a victory of civilization over barbarism. As acts of terrorism and the modalities of the spectacle converge, a new species of technological magic is produced in which shock becomes the structuring principle in creating certain conditions of reception for the images and discourses of terrorism and fear. Fear, as both an experience and a practice, has become the first principle in the spectacle of terrorism (though hardly its only principle); consequently, fear is now being used as a powerful force that flaunts an indifference to social justice while simultaneously working to distance audiences from any sense of critical engagement.

Violence, with its ever-present economy of organized fear, is no longer viewed or experienced merely as a side effect of war, greed, exclusion, and criminal behavior; it has become fundamental to a deliberate strategy of representation, marked by an excess of hyper-real visual displays of violence, in which the spectacle is central to a species of political rebirth that puts life back into a social order where only a vague and celluloid memory of consumption exists. Spectacular images of the "shock and awe" bombing of Baghdad by U.S. forces under President George W. Bush; the beheadings of hostages such as Nicholas Berg, Paul Johnson Jr., and *Wall Street Journal* reporter Daniel Pearl; the destruction of sixteenth-century mosques (as in Banja Luka, Bosnia) or of Buddhist statues (as in Bamiyan, Afghanistan)—all are intended to highlight and give legitimation to a reading of politics and agency in which more tactile categories such as fear, death, survival, life, and security replace the more abstract and modernist principles of truth, reason, and justice.[15] This is a politics in which violence becomes central to a war of images, and the spectacle becomes central to legitimating social relations in which the political and pedagogical are redefined in ways that undercut democratic freedom and practices. Mass and image-based media have become a new and powerful pedagogical force, reconfiguring the very nature of politics, cultural production, engagement, and resistance. Under such circumstances, it becomes all the more urgent for educators, artists, and citizens to develop a new set of theoretical tools to comprehend how visual representations of shockingly horrific violence are shaping the very nature of politics at a time when global media are conscripted into the worldwide war on terror. What might it mean to understand, engage, and transform the spectacle of terrorism as part of a broader struggle over the culture of politics, new media technologies, and democracy itself?

In what follows, I want to argue that while the merging of terror, violence, and screen culture has a long history, a new type of spectacle—the spectacle of terrorism—has emerged in the post-9/11 world, inaugurated by the video images of the hijacked planes crashing into the World Trade Center. This event, I suggest, not only signals a structural transformation in the pedagogical power of the image but also constitutes a space for a new kind of cultural politics. I begin this discussion by examining the changing nature of the spectacle in contemporary society, analyzing the spectacle of fascism and the spectacle of consumerism as two different expressions of what I call the *terror of the spectacle.* I then attempt to address the emergence of the *spectacle of terrorism* by focusing primarily on the emergence and popularity of one graphic instance of the spectacle of terrorism: the beheading videos that have been used by Iraqi insurgents in their attempts to resist Western occupation. I then argue that earlier discourses of the spectacle, from Guy Debord's classic definition to the recent work of Douglas Kellner,[16] while performing an important theoretical service in engaging the spectacle as a central aspect of cultural politics in the contemporary era, need to be revised so as to provide the theoretical tools required to fully understand how the spectacle has changed as a pedagogical and political practice since the first video images of fiery plane crashes and collapsing towers inaugurated the war on terror. My argument focuses on the idea that recent work linking state and nonstate violence, terrorism, and the state of exception cannot be fully understood without examining the relation between terrorism and security through the concept of the spectacle—a move that ultimately highlights in new and significant ways the issue and importance of new media and their productive moment as a form of cultural pedagogy and politics. I will conclude by exploring how the new fusion of media and technology might produce a new understanding of public pedagogy and a more critical conception of cultural politics.

Beyond the Spectacles of Fascism and Consumerism

The history of the spectacle is inextricably tied to the politics of illusion, seduction, pageantry, and exhibition. Voyeurism and fantasy work together through various representations and practices organized within diverse pedagogical sites to render subjects willing to surrender their potential as agents to the state and, more recently, the demands of the market. The pedagogical function of the spectacle is to promote consent (though it has also functioned coercively), integrate populations into dominant systems of power, heighten fear, and operate as a mode of social reproduction largely through the educational force of the broader culture. At the same time, the spectacle is about more than the organization of ideas, knowledge, images, and symbols; it also "refers to the vast institutional and technical apparatuses" available to different social orders engaging in a cultural politics designed to "relegate subjects passive, and obscure the nature and effects of capitalism's power and deprivations."[17] The spectacle is neither a universal nor a transcendental force haunting social relations. It emerges in different forms under distinct social formations, and signals in different ways how cultural politics works necessarily as a pedagogical force to produce subjects willing to serve the political and economic power of dominant groups. While the threat of state violence and terror has always been a distinct element of the spectacle, the degree to which such violence has become visible or actually employed has depended on the state's ability "to command obedience for the sake of peace, justice, prosperity, and reasonable expectations of security."[18]

The relationship between formations of power and particular practices of the terror of the spectacle can be seen in various social formations and theoretical discourses, and in the politics they have legitimated. Before briefly analyzing these different formations and the ideologies that characterize the nature of the spectacles that govern them, I want to define in general terms the distinction between what I call terror of the spectacle and the spectacle of the terror. The *terror of the spectacle* refers to older notions of the spectacle that are often associated with both fascist culture and late capitalism's culture of commodification. Fascism and consumer capitalism share some very general features of the terror of the spectacle. These include the use of the spectacle "to build consensus by invoking collective rituals that attempt to mobilize affective structures of identification."[19] Demanding a certain mode of attentiveness or gaze elicited through phantasmagoric practices, including various rites of passage, parades, pageantry, advertisements, and media presentations, the terror of the spectacle offers the populace a collective sense of unity that serves to integrate them into state power.[20] One consequence is that civic life is debased through the use of public spectacles in which visual symbols and visual culture work to aestheticize politics through affective appeals to the monumental, commercial, and heroic, denigrating rational debate, dialogue, and language in general. The political registers and ideological coordinates of the terror of the spectacle are often written on the large screens and surfaces of the cultural landscape, as in the pageantry of the Nazi rallies, the visual spectacle of consumer culture, and the simulacra of the age of neoliberal glitz and celebrity culture. The terror of the spectacle is also evident in the visual character of the postcards and rituals that mediated the lynching of African-Americans at a time when racist symbolism defined and legitimated barbaric social relations as part of the discourse of law and order. In all of these cases, the terror of the spectacle appeals to a sense of unity, whether racial, nationalistic, or market-based, and, in doing so, downplays matters of politics and power while pointing to a utopian future as a basis for unity and consent. Politics and power are not eliminated; they are simply hidden within broader appeals to solidarity. In short, the terror of the spectacle downplays a politics in which terror is central to its very definition of sovereignty, and the various anti-democratic relations being legitimated do not necessarily involve a form of politics and technological mediation in which the primacy of the visual demands the heightened spectacularity of war.

In contrast, the spectacle of terrorism as an expression of state and corporate power aims at creating a new notion of the subject forged in social relations largely constructed around fear and terror, legitimating a notion of sovereignty that "resides, to a large degree, in the power and the capacity to dictate" who is safe and who is not, who is worthy of citizenship and who is a threat, who can occupy the space of safety and who cannot, and ultimately "who may live and who must die."[21] Equally important, the spectacle of terrorism is not simply a new expression of state and corporate power; it is increasingly in open revolt against state and corporate power and posits a form of address that is both explicitly political and expressed primarily as "the right to kill," the right to embrace lawlessness as the defining space of the political, and the right to exercise "power outside of the law."[22] The spectacle of terrorism conjures up its meaning largely through the power of images that grate against humane sensibilities. Rather than indulging a process of depoliticization by turning consuming into the only responsibility of citizenship, the spectacle of terrorism politicizes through a theatrics of fear and shock. Moreover, the spectacle of terrorism is not simply about the "thrill of the illusion"; it is primarily about "the image added with the thrill of the real."[23] Under the auspices of the spectacle of terrorism, the small-screen culture of the television, camcorder, and computer asserts its power not only through a mastery of the image but also through a massive return to "the real" in which hyper-violence attempts to construct a subject and a public in a state of permanent fear as well as a world that is turned upside down, bereft of its traditional modernist, market-based coordinates.[24] The spectacle of terrorism undercuts the primacy of consumerism by adding to it,[25] challenges state power, and uses the image to construct a new type of politics organized around the modalities of death, hysteria, panic, and violence. But it does more. Mediated through the new image-based technologies, the spectacle of terrorism emerges as a central force not only in shaping social relations forged in the culture of fear and death but also in legitimating the very connection between terrorism and security.[26]

The terror of the spectacle and the spectacle of terrorism are neither completely divorced from each other nor suggestive of a complete historical break, in that they overlap and coexist. Elements of the terror of the spectacle such as the representational politics of consumerism are alive and well, and both regimes share a number of traits. These include mobilizing "people's feelings primarily to neutralize their critical senses, massaging minds and emotions so that the individual succumbs to the charisma of vitalistic power."[27] In addition, both regimes accentuate performative practices designed to foster unity in the interest of solidifying authoritarian ideologies, values, and identities.

Nevertheless, different social formations produce spectacles unique to particular historical periods. In the 1930s, the fascist spectacle was embodied in the theater of giganticism with its precisely scripted pageantry around "the massing of groups of people";[28] endless representations glorifying war, physical perfection, and virility posing as enlightened experiences; rallies accentuating the monumental and obedience to the heroic leader; art glorifying racial purity and uniformed white men; and mythological representations of ultranationalism. Allen Feldman captures this phenomenon in his analysis of the fascist political rally and the aestheticization of modern violence. He writes:

> The Fascist political rally was a theatre that incorporated the individual spectator into a virtualized corporate body of sovereignty. The construction of this virtual mass subject aligned political attention and a politics of suggestion with mass consumption aesthetics. This was mechanical reproduction in the service of a mythographic spectacle, in which violence was sold as a political commodity, as a binding media of crowd formation, and, through the cinematics of the mass rally, made palatable as a mechanized and routine efficacy. The aestheticization of modern violence was only possible through political technologies of suggestion and visually orchestrated mass consciousness, which conveyed perceptual agency to the screen, the lens and to the virtualized mass bodies that were integral to the spectacle of Fascist sovereignty.[29]

Under the gaze of mythological power and sovereignty, the fascist spectacle enabled modes of spectatorship that organized mass bodies through the production of politics as a form of theater and spectacle with a penchant for ceremonies and rituals and a paramilitary orientation. Wedded to a culture of spectacularized symbols, fascist imagery both masculinized the public sphere and infused it with a militaristic spirit "derived principally from the exultation of war as a space in which men can know themselves better and love one another legitimately in the absence of the feminine."[30] Transforming politics into aesthetics, the fascist spectacle energetically sought to destroy democratic notions of legality, morality, values, and justice. As both a political act and an instrument of power, the fascist spectacle turned individual and social experience into a projection of state power; in doing so, it destroyed any vestige of democratic solidarity, replacing it with a sutured community "that privileged cultic forms over ethical norms"[31] and favored vitalistic, authoritarian power over critical reflection and autonomous agency. Combining premodern sentiments with modern machines, the fascist spectacle stylized political action through a "seductive organization of public signs, meanings, and iconographies."[32] Merging the cult of violence with the technology of the broadcast media, fascist aesthetics and the political culture it produced were organized through a larger-than-life scale of illusion and transparency that was "possible only in the age of film, the gramophone and the loudspeaker."[33] Violence in the fascist spectacle was a unifying force for a "pure politics" that glorified the image of a belligerent ultra-nationalism and the state as a vitalistic military power, with its promise of triumphalism and empire; in addition, such violence was reproduced in the fascist adulation of the strong over the weak, evident not only in a commitment to racist ideology obsessed with purity but also in the militarization of public space, the celebration of "the armed and militarized political subject,"[34] and the mindless exaltation of sacrifice for the fatherland. As Paul Gilroy rightly argues, visual technologies in the service of the fascist spectacle both devalued speech as a medium of communication and allowed the public to move beyond the reflexive world of print culture to the culture of the screen in which the "national collective could discover and take pleasure in itself and its common subordination to an all-powerful leadership in equally novel ways."[35]

While the association between mid-century fascism and aesthetics, and by implication the spectacle, has been the subject of critical analysis by theorists as diverse as Walter Benjamin, Peter Burger, Martin Jay, Paul Gilroy, Susan Buck-Morss, and Lutz Koepnick, the most promising work on the politics of the spectacle and contemporary society has been organized around the relationship between the spectacle and the consumer society of late capitalism. Guy Debord, Hal Foster, Jean Baudrillard, and Douglas Kellner, among others, have not only greatly extended our knowledge of how the spectacle works in a variety of sites to reproduce the most central values and practices of consumer ideology; they have also raised crucial questions about how the concept and society of the spectacle might enable the United States to grasp the present age.

Guy Debord's pioneering work in *The Society of the Spectacle* provides a number of important theoretical insights for critically understanding the transformation of the spectacle under late capitalism. According to Debord, the spectacle that emerged under late capitalism represented a new form of state control that was quite different from, even as it bore the political trace of, the fascist spectacle. Debord viewed the spectacle as a product of the market and a new form of cultural politics. He believed that the spectacle represented a "new stage in the accumulation of capital [in which] more and more facets of human activity and elements of everyday life were being brought under the control of the market."[36]

Under late capitalism, the spectacle was reforged in the crucible of mass consumption and mass media, producing new modes of communication constitutive of everyday life. Although the spectacle is often viewed by the public as mere entertainment, disconnected from power and politics, Debord insisted that "[t]he spectacle is the self-portrait of power in the age of power's totalitarian rule over the conditions of existence."[37] New technological developments in communications established the mode of information as a category equally as important for reproducing social life as labor had been for Marxism. Moreover, the society of the spectacle was not a specialized element of social existence; it had become a constituting activity that refigured the very nature of common sense and social relations. According to Debord, the "whole of life [now] presents itself as an immense accumulation of spectacles. All that was once directly lived has become mere representation."[38] The educational force of the culture, whether "news or propaganda, advertising or the actual consumption of entertainment," had been transformed into a spectacle that "epitomizes the prevailing model of social life."[39] Debord rightly recognized that the dynamics of domination under late capitalism could no longer be explained exclusively through reference to the economic sphere and its exploitative mode and relations of production. Rejecting conventional Marxist notions of social reproduction, Debord followed the theoretical lead of Antonio Gramsci, the Frankfurt School, and other neo-Marxist theorists who argued that domination was secured increasingly through "a social relationship between people that is mediated by images,"[40] and that capitalism had successfully employed an image industry to transform commodities into appearances and history into staged events. Under such circumstances, the society governed by the spectacle "proclaims the predominance of appearances and asserts that all human life, which is to say all social life, is mere appearance."[41] Moreover, according to Debord, "any critique capable of apprehending the spectacle's essential character must expose it as a visible negation of life—and as a negation of life that has *invented a visual form for itself.*"[42] In Debord's theory, the media had become the quintessential space of late capitalism, and consumerism had become their legitimating ideology. Or, to cite Debord's famous quip, "the spectacle is capital accumulated to the point where it becomes image."[43] What is so crucial about Debord's theory is that it connects the state's investment in social reproduction to its commitment in, "and control of, the field of images—the alternative world conjured up by the new battery of 'perpetual emotion machines' of which TV was the dim pioneer and which now beckons the citizen every waking minute."[44] Not only was the world of images a structural necessity for capitalism; it also affirmed the primacy of the pedagogical as a crucial element of the political and made visible "the submission of more and more facets of human sociability—areas of everyday life, forms of recreation, patterns of speech, idioms of local solidarity ... [—] to the deadly solicitation (the lifeless bright sameness) of the market."[45]

If in Debord's theory the spectacle was tied to the colonization of everyday life, then it became operational through a merger of state and corporate power that had mutual interest both in controlling the images through which society represented itself and in producing a subject consistent with the needs of consumerism, the desires embodied by the commodity, and the values of the marketplace. Under late capitalism, state violence made its mark not only through the prisons, courts, police surveillance, and other criminalizing forces; it also waged a form of symbolic violence mediated by a regime of consumer-based images and staged events that narrowed individual and social agency to the dictates of the marketplace, reducing the capacity for human aspirations and desires to needs embodied in the appearance of the commodity. In Debord's words, "the spectacle is the bad dream of modern society in chains, expressing nothing more than its wish for sleep."[46] Consumer society had now become a "society of the spectacle," a society organized around a vast array of commodities, various image-making technologies to promote them, and numerous sites from which to circulate them. It was a civic culture and social order that seemed incapable of resisting the consumer ideology of the spectacle. For Debord, the "society of the spectacle" was a force for conformity, depoliticization, and passivity that relentlessly attempted to hijack any viable notion of critical engagement and resistance by reconstituting the educational force of the culture in the interests of late capitalism.

Debord's notion of the spectacle made a significant contribution in mapping a new form of control associated with the accumulation of capital; it made clear that the whole industry of leisure, consumption, entertainment, advertising, fantasy, and other pedagogical apparatuses of media culture had become crucial elements of control, and thus a primary condition of politics. Rather than arguing that commodities had become the *sine qua non* of domination, he insisted, as Eugene L. Arva points out, that "the system of mediation by representation (the world of the spectacle, if you wish) has come to bear more relevance than commodities themselves."[47] In doing so, Debord furthered our understanding that domination had to be analyzed as part of a politics of consent in which all aspects of social life were increasingly being shaped by the communication technologies under the control of corporate capital. Although Debord has been accused of overestimating the all-encompassing power of the spectacle, media, and other control mechanisms of late capitalism ("a permanent opium war"),[48] he did not harbor the politically crippling pessimism of the Frankfurt School. His groundbreaking work, *The Society of the Spectacle*, "reads, rather, as a warning against the paralysis of the senses, the lethargy of the mind, and the political inertia with which a primarily visually determined, visually accessible, and most visually livable reality threatens" any viable notion of the autonomous subject.[49] He rejected the dystopian notion of the totally administered society and consistently argued for developing forms of resistance that took seriously the conditions that connected individual and social agency to elements of critique and social transformation. For Debord, social freedom and collective struggle were impossible without self-emancipation and autonomy.

Yet, the enormous analytic burden of Debord's theory reveals itself in precisely that which, in a globalizing post-9/11 world, it cannot explain. As Lutz Koepnick points out, we now live in a "post-Fordist culture ... characterized by hybrid multimedia aggregates and diversified strategies of consumption."[50] Within this new era, technology and media merge, resulting in a massive cultural reorganization involving the production, distribution, and consumption of information and images. Not only has the old model of a monolithic system of media control and cultural reproduction been undermined by contemporary media and technologies such as the Internet, computers, digital cameras, and VCRs, but entirely new configurations of communication relations have emerged in which the production, control, and dissemination of information and images have become more decentered and the global flows of images less manageable by corporations and governments.[51] At the same time, new media with their diverse technological image-making landscape have produced a new type of consumer who is more technologically savvy and who uses such media in more complex ways. In this age of cultural technologies such as Tivo digital video recording, the Apple iPod, the Blackberry wireless handheld, the camcorder, and the camera-phone, modernist assumptions about time and space being homogeneous and fixed are no longer applicable. The relationship among time, space, and place has been both stretched and compressed. Speed refigures our ability to access information, appropriate images from around the globe, and communicate with people on the other side of the planet. Just as new cultural technologies make possible highly individualized forms of symbolic appropriation, the undiversified masses have given way to a diverse globalized public far removed from the homogeneous community of viewers and producers that was allegedly characteristic of the older broadcasting age of media. Of course, I am not suggesting that new media and technological developments have ushered in structural changes amounting to a democratization of the media. This perspective is as inaccurate as it is overly romantic. At the same time, any analysis of public space must take into account the effects, speed, rhythms of information and communication, real-time images, differential modes of control, and unprecedented power increasingly deployed by the new media.

Mark Poster suggests that as communication technologies bypass the first media era in which "a small number of producers" controlling "film, radio, and television sent information to a larger number of consumers, an entirely new configuration of communication relations has emerged."[52] The second age of media, which has developed in the last few decades, not only created new modes of appropriation and production but also radicalized the conditions for creating critical forms of social agency and resistance, while also making more democratic and ethical claims for the use of knowledge, information, and images. Radically new modes of communication and resistance based upon the new media are on full display in the global justice movements, in the emergence of bloggers holding corporate and government powers more accountable, and in the new kinds of cultural and political struggles waged by the Zapatistas, the Seattle protesters, and various new social movements held together through the informational networks provided by the Internet and the Web.[53] As Stanley Aronowitz points out, "The excluded can use image-making as a weapon for laying hold and grasping cultural apparatuses.... [P]lacing old forms in new frameworks changes their significance."[54] In analyzing opposition to the U.S. occupation of Iraq, James Castonguay also underscores the subversive potential of these new modes of agency and resistance. He writes: "Newer media of the Internet and the Web not only have afforded mainstream media such as WB and CNN new modes of representation but have also provided new opportunities for the expression of dissent, new avenues of distribution for audio and video, and alternative representations of war unavailable during previous major U.S. conflicts."[55] Multiple identities, values, desires, and knowledge are now formed through globe-trotting imagery, offering up new modes of agency and possibilities for critique and resistance. While arguments suggesting that media technologies such as the Internet constitute a new democratic public sphere may be vastly premature, the new electronic media have not entirely faulted on their potential for both multiplying sites of cultural production and offering "resources for challenging the state's coordination of mass culture."[56]

Debord could not have imagined either how the second media revolution would play out, with its multiple producers, distributors, and consumers, or how a post-9/11 war on terrorism would transform the shift, especially in the United States, from an emphasis on consumerism to an equally absorbing obsession with war and its politically regressive corollaries of fear, anxiety, and insecurity.[57] The economic, political, and social safeguards of modernity, however restricted, along with traditional spatial and temporal coordinates of experience, have been blown apart in the "second media age" as the spectacularization of fear and the increasing militarization of everyday life have become the principal cultural experiences shaping identities, values, and social relations.[58] Giorgio Agamben asserts that under the spectacle of terrorism, security not only dominates state activity but also creates the potential for a new kind of authoritarianism:

> Today we face extreme and most dangerous developments in the thought of security. In the course of a gradual neutralization of politics and the progressive surrender of traditional tasks of the state, security becomes the basic principle of state activity. What used to be one among several definitive measures of public administration until the first half of the twentieth century now becomes the sole criterion of political legitimation. The thought of security bears within it an essential risk. A state which has security as its sole task and source of legitimacy is a fragile organism; it can always be provoked by terrorism to become itself terroristic.[59]

Agamben is only partly right, and, as John Comaroff insists, a caveat is in order here. The mythic threat of terrorism and violent crime provides the state with the legitimating power to increase its security and militaristic directions, but the contemporary state also reproduces its authoritarian tendencies "through an equally central primary task—the funnelling of public funds into the private; hence its transformation into an institutional mechanism for licencing and franchising" all aspects of the public good.[60] Stanley Aronowitz elaborates on this issue by arguing that the core functions of the state have shifted, not disappeared:

> Contrary to some recent arguments, the nation-state has not disappeared; instead its core functions have shifted from the legitimating institutions such as those of social welfare to, on the one hand, providing the monetary and fiscal conditions for the internal, but spurious expansion of (fictitious) capital, among whose elements is a reverse redistributive program, and on the other, to supplying a vastly expanded regime of coercion, that is, the growth of the police powers of government at home and abroad directed against the insurgencies that object to the growing phenomenon of an authoritarian form of democracy.[61]

A "state of emergency" exercised under the banner of the "war on terrorism," the primacy of neoliberal market values at all costs, and the legitimating principle of "permanent war" have trumped not only an atrophied democratic polis but also its nemesis: the primacy of the spectacle of consumerism. The consolidation of increasingly authoritarian state power in public life supersedes even the glitz of the suburban shopping mall—now reconceived as a tantalizing target for terrorist activity.[62] Enabled by the old and new media, a new kind of postmodern fear now haunts the United States in the contemporary era—a fear that is inextricably tied to the spectacle of terrorism and the move toward a new state of emergency. Francois Debrix's commentary on the production of emergency cultures captures the mood of this shift:

[A] generalized, illogical, and often unspecified sense of panic is facilitated in this postmodern environment where all scenarios can and often are played out. This generalized panic is no longer akin to the centralized fear which emanates from the power of the sovereign in the modern era. Rather, it is an evanescent sentiment that anything can happen anywhere to anybody at anytime. This postmodern fear is not capable of yielding logical, reasonable outcomes. All it does instead is acceler- ate the spiralling vortex of media-produced infor- mation. All it does is give way to emergencies (which will only last until the next panic is unleashed). This panic, I believe, is the paroxysmic achievement of media power.[63]

A number of theorists have attempted both to build upon the work of Debord and to render a more complex theoretical understanding of how the spectacle itself has changed, particularly in light of the emergence of new mass and image-based media technologies, the global advance of religious fundamentalisms, and the tragic events of September 11, 2001.[64] Douglas Kellner's work is particularly important and deserves some discussion. Kellner has written extensively on the notion of the spec- tacle and concludes, in agreement with Debord, that the spectacle of late capitalism has essentially taken over the conduct of the social. But Kellner's work expands the implications of Debord's theories. Kellner is less concerned with an abstract notion of the spectacle designed to map the general workings of capitalist society than he is with charting and engaging a range of distinct and specific examples of media spectacles that have mushroomed in the last few decades.[65] Kellner thus charts what is, in his view, a new stage in the development of the spectacle, one that demands an understanding of the new technologies making such spectacles possible as well as the implications of oppositional practices used against new forms of the spectacle. While Kellner believes that contemporary society is "saturated with spectacles, ranging from daily 'photo opportunities,' to highly orchestrated special events which dramatize state power, to TV ads and image management for competing candidates,"[66] he argues that it is imperative to recognize the distinctive character of such spectacles as well as the novel spaces and sites in which they occur. Accordingly, Kellner examines how spectacles—understood now in their plurality and diversity—are played out in a variety of cultural and social formations such as sports, Hollywood films, television, contemporary architecture, schools, and global media, thereby providing a new language for recognizing the distinctive character of what he calls the megaspectacle, the interactive spectacle, and the political spectacle.[67]

According to Kellner, the *megaspectacle* is illustrated in events such as the O. J. Simpson trial and the Bush "war on terrorism" and has the distinctive quality of not only defining certain eras but also driving mainstream media culture. The second form of spectacle, which he labels as *interactive,* refers to those cultural forms and technologies in which audiences talk back, interact with each other, and shape particular modes of communication. This type of interaction can be seen in television shows where audiences vote to decide the outcome of an event or contest; it can also be seen in Internet dating, video games, distance education, and virtual-reality technologies. Another spectacle, which he categorizes as *political,* is evident in events such as the Persian Gulf TV War as well as the U.S. occupation of Iraq under George W. Bush.[68] Such events are played out endlessly in the media in ways that sensationalize (shock and awe) even as they drain from such events any viable ethical and political substance.

Kellner's focus is on the emergence of new spectacles, the kinds of ideological and political work they do, and the specific sites in which they take place. Whereas Debord understood the spectacle primarily as a way of criticizing late capitalism, Kellner's approach is "more interpretative and interrogatory."[69] For instance, rather than simply examining how McDonald's and Nike use the spectacle as part of an attempt to market their products and lure consumers, Kellner examines what "McDonald's tells us about consumption and the consumer society, or globalization; what Michael Jordan and the Nike spectacle tell us about the sports spectacle and the intersection of sports, entertainment, advertising, and commodification in contemporary societies."[70] Kellner's analysis of the spectacle differs from Debord's in that he is unwilling to concentrate exclusively on how the spectacle works to promote passivity, facilitate domination, and depoliticize the populace. Kellner is also concerned with the internal contradictions that characterize spectacles and with the questions of how to identify their oppositional moments and how new media might be used politically to foster new forms of understanding about hegemony and to develop new tools for resistance. Both Kellner and Debord, among others, have greatly advanced our understanding of the political and pedagogical significance of the spectacle in the contemporary era, but the invaluable theoretical insights they provide cannot be stretched far enough to illuminate how the intersection of violence, terror, and the media has produced yet another complicated twist in the drama of the spectacle, one that offers a distinctively different set of ideological and political registers for grasping its effects on both the contemporary and the future shape of media and the broader global public sphere.

The distinctive mark of the gruesome and horrible attacks on the Twin Towers and the Pentagon is that they were designed to be visible, designed to be spectacular. They not only bear an eerie similarity to violence-saturated Hollywood disaster films but are similarly suited to—intended for—endless instant replay on the nightly news, bringing an end to democratic freedoms with democracy's blessings. The attacks were clearly predicated on the assumption that "a picture is worth a thousand words—that a picture in the present condition of politics is itself, if sufficiently well-executed, a specific and effective piece of statecraft."[71] In retrospect, the events of 9/11 not only redefined the relationship between the power of the media and the politics of the social imaginary; they also ushered in a new kind of politics, one tied to a new notion of the spectacle that no longer works in the service of the state, however a state might appropriate it. I want to suggest that this emerging spectacle of terrorism is quite different from the fascist spectacles and the spectacle of consumerism. The spectacles employed in the interests of both fascism and late capitalism functioned largely to promote different versions of control in the service of state domination. Both used fear as an implicit threat, and both worked to emphasize the spectacle as a force for unification over genuine political participation. Since September 11, 2001, a different type of spectacle has emerged in which fear and terror become its most salient organizing principles, and politics reveals itself through the raw display of power and brutal violence. Not only is the state an object rather than the subject of terrorist spectacles; the origins of such attacks are also bereft of state organization and legitimation. I am not suggesting that the state does not engage in terrorist acts mediated through the aesthetic of violence. Actually, this has become commonplace in recent times. What I am arguing is that the "definition of politics as the warlike relation par excellence"[72] is no longer exercised merely by the state but also through relations forged outside of its control and that, in the present historical moment, the vulnerability of state sovereignty and the possibility of stateless sovereignty have, in part, enabled the ascendancy of fundamentalist religious authority throughout the globe.

Image-Based Media and the Spectacle of Terrorism

Before I elaborate on the distinctive characteristics of the spectacle of terrorism and its implications for connecting critical pedagogy and cultural politics, I want to highlight the changing nature of the spectacle in contemporary society by analyzing the images being mobilized within the aesthetic of mass-mediated violence. In doing so, I want to demonstrate briefly how the spectacle of terrorism complicates previous theories of the spectacle, defined almost exclusively through the merging of mass consumption and its multi-mediated images of endless attainable pleasures. Unlike Guy Debord's society of the spectacle, which justifies capitalism by elevating consumption to an aesthetic ur-experience, the spectacle of terrorism affirms politics (of war, life, sacrifice, and death) over the aesthetics of commodification through an appeal to the real over the simulacrum. The spectacle of terrorism also points to the reemergence of older forms of control and persuasion that operate outside of and differently from the modernist forms of disciplinary control and bio-politics exercised through surveillance, the courts, the military, schools, hospitals, and the police, and made legible by Michel Foucault. Moreover, the spectacle of terrorism capitalizes on a notion of subjectivity and identity that is troubled in a world where meaning appears to have collapsed, building social consensus around fear rather than consumption and substituting a compassion for the other with a fear for oneself. The spectacle of terrorism has colonized the gaze and imagination of millions of people, especially as it emerges in a flood of images that bypass traditional sites of power such as dominant television networks and newspaper outlets. Against a media saturated with images of American violence against Muslims legitimated on political and religious grounds, the insurgent-produced videos and images provide a means of response and a measure of revenge in the Arab world.

Removed from any conventional notions of normativity, the spectacle of terror trades on our inability to "look away from representations of diseased or damaged bodies, from excremental objects, from the staged decompositions of life that have become central to contemporary aesthetic practice—we are, in a sense, staring into the dimension of 'bare life' that uncannily persists in its exclusion from any normativity, from any form of life."[73] And it is precisely this affective structure of identification, with a viscerally moving presence of elemental fear, suffering, abjection, degradation, and death, that ties us to a retrograde notion of the social that is organized around a culture of shared fears rather than shared responsibilities. Such staring, however, may ultimately be part of what sustains our affective bond to the existing state of authoritarian social relations. The spectacle of terrorism cannot be thought of or grasped without a recognition of the growing public fascination with and proliferation of a series of globally distributed images that include footage of the two hijacked planes crashing into the World Trade Center in Manhattan, the pornographic representations of abuse and torture at Abu Ghraib prison, the brutal execution of Nicholas Berg, the beheading of *Wall Street Journal* reporter Daniel Pearl by al-Qaeda terrorists, the endless images shown on Fox News celebrating U.S. military operations in Iraq, and the Osama bin Laden propaganda videos.

In the war of images, video technology has become a primary tool used by terrorists to distribute images, including speeches by terrorist leaders, gruesome beheadings, jihadist hip-hop music videos, and suicide bombers using cell phones to document their own deaths, and also to bear witness to the victims of state terrorism as in the images of Muslims being killed by American and British soldiers. The Internet, too, has become a powerful tool for airing streaming videos and images that include everything from Arabs experiencing indignities at the hands of American soldiers, especially the images of the torture and abuse of detainees at Abu Ghraib prison, to Israeli soldiers abusing Palestinians. Gary Bunt uses the term *Cyber Jihad* to describe how adept the Iraqi insurgents have become both in manipulating the Internet and in getting their messages out to domestic and international audiences.[74] The terrorist videos—which are sold on the street, distributed to television networks, and posted on the Internet—address a range of audiences and cover a diverse number of activities, including statements recorded by suicide bombers, tributes to deceased fighters, and documentary images of insurgents engaged in military operations such as shooting mortars or launching land-to-air missiles.

The most popular videos, the ones that have had the greatest effect on target audiences, are the gruesome beheading and execution videos.[75] Here, hostages are generally seen blindfolded and kneeling on the ground, surrounded by Islamic militants who sometimes precede the execution with political statements or demands read in Arabic. The hostages are usually forced to identify themselves and sometimes prodded to plead pitilessly for their lives before the camera. The beheadings are remarkably grisly, often carried out with long, serrated knives. Recent videos exhibit as many as ten executions at a time.

I have argued that the new regime of the spectacle is distinct from that of consumer society; yet, it is ironic that the spectacle of terrorism appears perfectly matched for media constantly in search of higher ratings. And while established networks will not air the actual beheadings, they provide enormous coverage of hostage-takings and kidnappings by terrorists groups. As Ibrahim al-Marashi points out, the "videos of kidnapped hostages have proved successful in forcing world leaders to withdraw troops from Iraq, preventing international firms from participating in reconstruction efforts, and instigating rallies against the occupation of Iraq in the hostages' countries. Therefore, however repugnant is the footage, it constitutes a success for the insurgents in attracting world attention to their cause."[76] The implications of the political and market success of the videos cannot be overstated.

While dominant groups have a long history of merging politics and aesthetics to impose state power, the media and technologies of the current era enable new forms of resistance in that the war of images is no longer exclusively controlled by dominant Western powers or used entirely by the state against its declared enemies. Increasingly, political struggles are being waged, and power refined, through the manipulation of images by stateless groups engaged in oppositional struggles. One measure of the success that the spectacle of terrorism provides for oppositional groups can be seen in the popularity of their videos. For instance, Hamza Hendawi reports that, in Baghdad, "real-life horror has become the view fare of choice, supplanting the explosion of pornography that filled the post–Saddam Hussein vacuum."[77] In outdoor food markets in Baghdad, crowds gather to watch "video footage of a truck bomber seated behind the steering wheel smiling and murmuring his last words before crashing into U.S. military vehicles on an overpass."[78] As the public executions, assassinations, and beheadings continue in Iraq, they are followed by an endless stream of videos that can be purchased as DVDs in local markets, some for as little as thirty cents apiece. Ibrahim al-Marashi reports that

> [v]ideos of insurgent attacks against Coalition Forces as well as the beheadings of foreigners have proven to be fast-selling "entertainment" in Iraq, implying that sympathy for these acts exists. The sale of video discs featuring hostages being executed by Islamic militants was banned by the Iraqi police, yet still make up 75 percent of the domestic movie vendors' sales, indicating that Iraqis are aware of the insurgents' capabilities for sowing fear in Iraq, if not approving the insurgents' actions.[79]

In fact, images of death and torture are not only sold in Baghdad and other parts of the Arab world; they are also viewed online across the globe and have been sold in the United States. According to one report, a convenience store in Tampa, Florida, stocked its shelves with a DVD titled *Buried in the Sand*, which shows some of the gruesome torture Saddam Hussein handed out to his enemies and also "prominently features the end of Nicholas Berg's life—in all, a series of brutally graphic, violent images culminating with the beheading."[80] Thus, as Matthew McAllester points out, "it is not just Iraqis who are keen to see the films, Internet users all over the world appear to be satisfying their curiosity online by watching the same videos, which often are released by the kidnappers after they have killed their hostages."[81] Images of fear, shock, and hate are now global, posted on Internet sites, recorded on DVDs, captured on videos and sold to the general public, appearing in a multitude of public spaces, including Internet cafés. Dan Klinker, a Dutchman who runs a site that makes available the video beheadings, claims that "[d]uring tragic events like beheadings, the amount of visitors can rise up to 750,000 a day."[82] While beheadings and other insurgent images are increasingly viewed on various screens around the globe, the war of images is not limited to decapitation videos. Digital video cameras, fax machines, and photographs are now also employed as part of the spectacle of terrorism, increasingly used by marginalized groups and insurgents to fight a new kind of war against state power with its arsenal of conventional bombs, helicopters, tanks, guns, and soldiers.

In combining a premodern form of punishment with the commandeering of a modern medium, the insurgents in Iraq have not only created a strategy for tapping into a powerful source of collective fear but also used the new electronic technologies to recruit young Muslims to join the Iraqi insurrection in the name of an authentic and original Islam. Upping the terror quotient, the insurgents use the media to instill fear in the West by graphically portraying a mutilating brutality that goes beyond the act of murder and, at the same time, makes a claim, however false and preposterous, for a "traditional" Islam, authenticated by a mode of execution with the sword that suggests a value-system close to the roots of Islam. Sinan Salaheddin is right in insisting that "behind the mix of brutality, adeptly produced video and a free global distribution system, the militants are tapping into a network of fears many centuries old—and blending the ancient with the modern to create a freshly powerful method of communication."[83]

But the new technologies do more than serve as recruitment videos, instill "shock and awe," and make visible the rituals of humiliation imposed on Muslims

and Arabs by occupying forces; they also become a potent political weapon in which images of terror are used
as part of a strategy to make demands against Western
nations, demands that extend from a call for ransom
money to requests that particular countries, such as Ita-
ly and the Philippines, withdraw their workers or troops
from Iraq. In addition, the videos serve as a key weapon
in spreading the message that the United States can be
defeated in Iraq and that the forces of the Coalition of
the Willing are not impregnable, just as the images of the
terrorist attacks on the World Trade Center are played
over and over again on the Internet and on television,
reinforcing both the vulnerability of the West and the
possibility of defeat through new technologies and tactics. These videos situate the body both as an object of
abuse and torture and as an agent of resistance. Against
the biopolitics of Western sovereignty with its power to
instill dread in the enemy by exercising absolute control
over life and death, the suicide bomber, in particular,
presents a direct challenge to such control and affirms
the body as a weapon that brazenly proclaims that "the
power over life and death that the sovereign exercises
becomes useless."[84]

Most of the commentary on the videos by American
news outlets focuses on the sheer brutality of the execution videos. Talk radio fills the airwaves with an inces-
sant outrage against the beheadings but offers little, if
any, analysis of either the conditions that produce them
and their rampant popularity or what they suggest about
how the nature of the political is being refigured within
the new media and the realm of the virtual.[85] Other
commentators cite the beheadings and propaganda
videos to condemn the primitiveness of the insurgents

and their tactics. For instance, Paul Marshall, writing for the *Weekly Standard,* sees in the beheadings Muslim fanatics waging an "apocalyptic war [in order] to purge the world of all but their version of Islam."[86] Many commentators are both disturbed by and critical of viewers who access the Internet to watch such videos. For example, Ted Koppel, on the television program *Nightline,* expressed moral outrage over people who downloaded the beheading videos from the Internet, suggesting that, when viewed, such images coarsen our moral indifference to violence.[87] Cultural critic Neal Gabler argues a different position, asserting that the running dialectic between moral outrage (pain) and pleasure has little to do with the public consumption of beheading videos. He insists that images of beheadings are popular because they play "to an emerging sensibility that regards finding and then watching these images not as horrors to be shunned or terrible realities to be viewed but as pieces of information one must see because not to see them is to be left out.... It is less voyeurism than a kind of validation.... Not to know is to be condemned to eternal geekdom."[88] Gabler's position is all too typical of the refusal of many commentators to combine moral outrage with serious analysis. Michael Ignatieff, a defender of U.S. policies in Iraq, hints at such analysis by claiming that the videos represent a new vital weapon in framing atrocities as images that arouse the curiosity of audiences while simultaneously instilling in them a profound sense of fear.[89] Commenting on the way in which the camera has become an instrument of terror, Ignatieff writes:

> The Chechen rebels seem to have been the first to film these grotesque parodies of Islamic justice.

Now there is a market in such bloody spectacles, with criminal gangs supplying the crucial actors: abducting foreigners in Iraq and selling them to terrorist groups like Abu Musab al-Zarqawi's Tawhid and Jihad. Terrorists have been quick to understand that the camera has the power to frame a single atrocity and turn it into an image that sends shivers down the spine of an entire planet. This gives them a vital new weapon.[90]

For Ignatieff, the war of images waged by Iraqi insurgents constitutes a different kind of politics in which narratives of mortification at the hands of the occupying powers fuel a new sense of entitlement among radical Muslims who can rationalize that everything is permitted and "that in an occupied country there are no innocent foreigners."[91] In this instance, the spectacle of terrorism is nourished by acts of revenge in which all the standard ethical concerns and legalistic norms of waging war simply disappear. Ignatieff is most concerned about the political effects of the spectacle of terrorism, arguing that it threatens to shatter American will in Iraq and force the American public into a kind of cynicism in which moral disgust will hasten U.S. withdrawal from Iraq rather than motivate the American public to continue the fight. In short, he views any withdrawal from Iraq as a failure of moral nerve. But in taking such a narrow view of either evil or justice, he undermines his own attempts to engage the spectacle of terrorism as having a political significance that goes far beyond the specificity of the war in Iraq, particularly as it narrowly relates to American interests. In the end, Ignatieff fails in his attempt to understand the larger political implications of the war of images, dismissing it simply as a form of evil that demands severe condemnation in an effort to strengthen the "moral" fortitude required to continue a war that has brought about the violent deaths of about 25,000 Iraqi civilians and the maiming of over 42,000 in the two years following the U.S.-led invasion.[92]

While many commentators and theorists have written about the images and cultural politics of abuse, torture, and brutal killings that have emerged from the battle-worn landscape of Iraq, there has been little commentary on how the spectacle of terrorism that mediates such acts is able to reach and affect diverse audiences in a multitude of pedagogical sites. There are very few critical and sustained attempts to understand the spectacle of terrorism within the changing conditions of the new information age with its integration of electronic, satellite, and digital technologies, and its enormous power to influence multiple producers and consumers.[93] The camcorders, digital cameras, and television screens provide unprecedented levels of public access and display. The new media, largely available through the mediation of the screen, occupy an ever larger social space—an insight not limited to its use by Iraqi insurgents. For instance, the Iraqi government has attempted to counter the popularity of the insurgents' war of images by producing their own reality-based television show called *Terrorism in the Grip of Justice.*[94] The show, which airs twice a day, features an ongoing series of confessions by captured insurgents. The government appropriates the spectacle of terrorism in order to "win the hearts and minds of the Iraqi people"[95] through a war of images, peddling fear as part of the larger discourse of security and government control. In this instance, a daily ritual of confessions and humiliation is played out as part of a scripted presentation in which "[m]artial music and images of mosques and other holy sites are interspersed with scenes of violence at the beginning of each broadcast. The Shiite Muslim call to prayer accompanies the opening of the daytime showing; the slightly different Sunni version of the prayer plays at night."[96]

Similar reality-based examples of how the new digital technologies are used to expand the realm of the pedagogical and political through the power of the image and screen culture can also be found in the United States. For instance, police in Baltimore discovered a DVD titled *Stop Snitching,* produced by drug dealers who "threatened to kill anyone who testified against them."[97] Local thugs appear in the video, pulling guns from their waistband and threatening anyone in the neighborhood who might report their drug activity to the police. The police responded with a DVD of their own called *Keep Talking,* which not only provided anonymous-tip phone lines and pictures of suspected drug dealers but also inaugurated a new use of police videos to communicate directly with both the criminals and the law-abiding citizens of Baltimore. While previous conceptions of the spectacle were almost entirely linked to entertainment, pageantry, parades, broadcast media, and various visual strategies used by dominant powers to garner consent from the populace, the new spectacle of terrorism complicates the relationship between audio-visual culture and politics, with no guarantees that the new technologies cannot be redeployed against state power itself. This is evident not only in the infamous example of the Rodney King video, in which a digital camcorder recorded an insidious act of police brutality and was used eventually to convict the police officers involved in the crime, but also more recently when a gruesome video was made public showing Serbian soldiers killing Bosnian Muslims in the town of Srebrenica. This video provided the Serbian public, only half of whom believed the massacre of eight thousand Muslims at Srebrenica actually took place, with graphic and direct evidence of the crimes committed by a Serbian unit known as the Scorpions, who "were under the command of the Serbian interior ministry."[98] Once the television broadcast of the video was widely viewed, Serbian President Boris Tadic issued a public assurance that the perpetrators of the crime would be punished.

The impact of the spectacle resulting from acts of state terrorism forces issues of accountability and responsibility to the fore; a traumatized segment of the citizenry achieves justice. But how does one account for the lure of such videos by others? Another structural element that characterizes the spectacle of terrorism and accounts for its power as a pedagogical force is the way in which it offers up images that resonate with cultural memories and forms of experience that are tied to specific, rather than general, sensibilities and lived events. With its focus on the real, mediated primarily through images of death, violence, and human suffering, the spectacle of terrorism carries with it an emotional truth that words alone cannot match. In addition, the emotional intensity of images of horror and torture becomes more meaningful when such images articulate with particular kinds of memories that give them a resonance, suggesting that the specific kinds of vulnerability and fear they are mobilizing cannot simply be defined within some kind of generalization. The memories associated with these images provide a power and resonance for different groups that cannot be overlooked. For example, the videotapes displaying the gruesome beheading of *Wall Street Journal* reporter Daniel Pearl cannot stand alone as simply a general instance of horror since they exist within a larger set of discourses and narratives that are part of an ongoing cultural memory and extended legacy in Jewish history.[99] State-supported violence such as pogroms and the Holocaust are part of the legacy of memories that both inform and are activated by the Pearl videotape. The Pearl video is also part of an expanding discussion in Jewish circles about the escalation of violence and new forms of anti-Semitism that are emerging around the world. There is a further concern that the production of anti-Semitism has shifted from the West to the Middle East, where television programs, newspaper articles, and religious clerics are calling for the destruction of Israel and the killing of Jews. But the Pearl video cannot be understood within a singular narrative of remembrance; rather, it has to be seen as a part of duelling memories and discourses of appropriation. For instance, the Pearl videotape has also been used by Islamic fundamentalists as testimony to the power of their movement and "the Pearl body as a rhetorical condensation of America, of Jewishness, of Zionism; the Pearl body is, metaphorically speaking, America."[100] In other instances, the U.S. media often used the Pearl video to justify a rather virulent brand of nationalist rhetoric while the Bush administration used it to justify its war against terrorism.

There is little awareness in commentaries such as Ignatieff's that the terror foregrounded in these images and videos resonates powerfully with a range of ideologies, issues, and cultural memories that mark contemporary life in the neoliberal landscape of American society. Hence, the spectacular attacks of September 11th on the major symbol of capitalism (the World Trade Center) and the center of militarism (the Pentagon) can, in part, be understood as reinforcing a general sense of fear and insecurity brought on by market volatility and the frenzy of downsizing; but more specifically, they resonate with a set of historical conditions in which a new vulnerability has emerged regarding the inability of the state to protect its citizens from both foreign terrorists and larger economic disasters. The images that often drive the spectacle of terrorism appeal to notions of vulnerability and perceived threats that have become commonplace since the tragic events of September 11th and have been consistently heightened by government manipulation of public sentiment, particularly in the United States, as part of the "war against terrorism." The alienation many people feel in an utterly privatized and individualized market society is exacerbated within a government- and media-produced culture of fear, suggesting that the terror we face at home and abroad cannot be fought without surrendering one's sense of agency and social justice to a militarized state. That has made war the primary organizing principle of the social order and all relations of power.[101] The mass circulation in the Arab world of the suicide bomber's videotape, images of abuse and torture of Arab and Muslim detainees at Abu Ghraib, and videotapes depicting violent acts of sabotage against American troops cannot be dismissed simply as a morbid fascination with violence. In many cases, these images articulate powerfully with memories drawn from Muslim resistance in the face of Soviet oppression in

Afghanistan, the struggle of the Palestinians against Israeli state terrorism, and various opposition movements against the presence of the United States in the Middle East under both Bush regimes.

Any critical attempt to engage the spectacle of terrorism must take place within a broader understanding of how the new media and electronic technologies have merged with the war on terror in both its state-sanctioned form and its role as a tool of insurgency and opposition to state power, particularly the power of the United States and its allies. The new media technologies coupled with the logic of permanent war have helped to redefine the very conditions that make politics possible. Central to a post-9/11 politics are the elements of a growing authoritarianism, in which religious and political orthodoxies have come together in different ways to undermine any vestige of democracy as a force for global change. Politics in Iraq and Israel, for instance, are increasingly linked to the ideology of violence, revenge, occupation, and exclusion. In the United States, the weak notion of citizenship demanded by a market-based, commodity-driven society has given way to a version of the overzealous citizen-soldier obsessed with "American military power as the truest measure of national greatness"[102] and enthralled with military action as a central feature of patriotism. Evidence of the latter can be seen in the public support for vigilantism along the Mexican border, packaged in the patriotic theme of "minute men."

The dominant media do more than monopolize the symbolic field in ways typically compatible with state interests; they also promote a certain version of endemic danger and insecurity, consistently mobilizing the deepest impulses of people's vulnerability, while reinforcing the military, security, and surveillance functions of the state. As Agamben argues, "In the end, security and terrorism may form a single deadly system, in which they justify and legitimate each other's actions."[103] Under such circumstances, the spectacle of terrorism posits protection in the form of a risk-free environment as the defining demand of citizenship and lends political credence and ideological legitimacy to state authoritarianism.[104] Under the aegis of the terror of the spectacle, identities and desires were packaged for consumption, while actual violence was edited out of the script and displaced onto former colonial states, transformed into free-trade zones, and made plentiful in countries such as Indonesia, China, Vietnam, and the Philippines.[105] In contrast, the spectacle of terrorism confronts the subject not with the obligations of consumption but with a fear about her own freedom, a freedom that is now a permanent task rather than a right. My point here is not that the spectacle of consumerism is no longer operative or less potent but, rather, that the conditions which enabled it to monopolize public consciousness no longer exist; that is, populations can no longer afford to buy into its fantasy-driven logic. As larger segments of the working and middle classes become utterly disposable, the spectacle of terrorism takes hold within the context of an emergent carceral state, one based on fear and promoted through the spectacle of inequality and terrorism.[106]

On both sides of the war on terror, violence and redemption are now tied to each other within religiously and politically inspired world views that are utterly Manichean in their adherence to moral absolutes, represented through the binarisms of good and evil, pure and polluted, sacred and profane, and white and black. In a society that believes security is more important than democratic freedoms, officially sanctioned panic associated with the war on terrorism begins to mimic the primordial appeal of fear produced by fundamentalists and insurgents who use stark, apocalyptic images of destruction, suffering, and loss as the main currency of political culture. Under such circumstances, the "war" against the terror of occupation, the threat of suicide bombers, and the horrible beheadings carried out by ruthless fundamentalist thugs run the risk of being transformed into a war against justice itself, as civil liberties are suspended, civilians are killed, lands are seized, and violence becomes the only politics available. Within an ever-expanding global war zone, it becomes difficult for many people to engage images and information outside of the boundaries defined by the spectacle of terrorism. In this instance, the political overshadows the aesthetic and, in doing so, makes an appeal to a reality in which fear becomes the only currency through which one can define agency, politics, others, and one's relationship to the landscape of politics, freedom, and justice. Contrary to Baudrillard's formulation, the representation of politics has not disappeared into the vortex of the simulacra; it has been resurrected through the spectacle of terrorism in ways that sanction a renewed commitment to authoritarianism, to organizing public pedagogy as a central force for containing democratic values, and to promoting a view of the social defined almost exclusively through shared apprehension and distrust. Politics as the struggle over power, meaning, identities, and values has been moved into the sphere of the symbolic, practiced largely through the spectacle of terrorism. The state now performs itself, drawing its association with violence and force as the very condition of both government and politics.[107] In this instance, reality doesn't so much disappear as become mediated through different regimes of images, which, in turn, increasingly become a crucial "key to social power."[108]

What is especially disturbing about this war of images is that it is not only being shaped by a state-driven politics that reinforces the reckless polarities between terrorist and victims; it is also being utilized by diverse terrorist groups mired in the most narrow and life-threatening political and religious orthodoxies. The latter orthodoxy leaves no room for the free play of interpretation or dialogue, thus prohibiting the exercise of critical thought and transforming citizens into automatons.

In the United States, the war against terrorism, with its requisite pedagogy of fear dominating every conceivable media outlet, creates the conditions for transforming a weak American democracy into a dangerous authoritarian state. The pedagogical force of culture is now writ large within circuits of global transmission that defy both the military power of the state while simultaneously reinforcing the state's reliance on military power to respond to the external threat and to control its citizens. As I have mentioned previously, insurgents use digital video cameras to defy official power, recruit members to battle occupying forces, and to spread their doctrine of fear and religious orthodoxy. State power responds with the increased use of military force abroad and images of fear and terror—as well as an expanding carceral apparatus—at home. But the spectacle of terrorism not only returns us to the reality of violence and the spread of authoritarianism as the emerging condition of contemporary politics; it also posits a notion of the social, stripped of any democratic substance. As part of the war for and against terror, the importance of social life has emerged once again along-side the demand for security, but has been now largely defined, as Mary Kaldor insists, through a relationship between violence and politics in which "rather than politics being pursued through violent means, violence becomes politics. It is not conflict that leads to war but war itself that creates conflict."[109]

As the realm of the social becomes synonymous with the mutually determining relations of politics and vio-lence, there is not only a massive retreat from demo-cratic public cultures but also the emergence of a notion of the social in which politics is increasingly constituted outside of the law and the boundaries of democracy itself. As the spectacle of terrorism assaults individual subjects by administering visceral images of shock and fear to the body politic, the elemental democratic structures of the social become dysfunctional; conse-quently, the social opens up to a new space of politics that serves to consolidate power in the form of either the authoritarian state or the perceived securities of fundamentalist social formations, such as the church, mosque, or military.

Resisting the Spectacle of Terrorism

By way of conclusion, I want to argue that the spectacle of terrorism not only requires a new conception of politics, pedagogy, and society; it also raises significant questions about the new media and its centrality to democracy. The spectacle of terrorism and the conditions that have produced it do not sound the death knell of democracy, but raise fundamental questions about how we can "begin to rethink democracy from within these conditions."[110] Before offering a tentative and, by necessity, incomplete response to the broad question of how to imagine a new politics that addresses some of the pressing challenges of the current era, I want to examine the specific implications of engaging the critical role of the new media technologies in a time of permanent war. Two of the central questions posed by the challenge of the new media that have to be raised by citizens, students, educators, and cultural critics is how might "our hope for justice ... go through this technological circuit that constitutes the new media and the realm of the virtual.... [How might we] account for the differences between writing and e-mail, dissemination and the Internet, in terms of how it is both received and how it structures traditional subjects and objects in new ways"?[111] That is, how might these new technologies be used to put into place modes of identity, subjectivity, and agency that expand and deepen the possibilities of democracy rather than shut it down? How might these technologies be used to enable subjects to recognize how they are being constituted through the spectacles of terrorism and consumerism, and what might it mean to reject the commodified and anti-democratic forms of agency they are being offered through the new media? Most important, how might educators, artists, and other cultural workers work together to construct a cultural politics based on social relations that enable individuals and social groups to rethink the crucial nature of pedagogy, agency, and social responsibility in a media-saturated global sphere? In addition, what might it mean to address these new technologies within a democratic cultural politics that challenges religious fundamentalism, neoliberal ideology, militarism, and the cult of entertainment?

At stake here is more than a pedagogical practice that protects texts and images from being absorbed into the spectacle of terrorism, as well as into other forms of the spectacle. Instead, pedagogy becomes central to developing those ideologies and skills needed to critically understand the new visual and visualizing technologies and their attendant screen culture, not simply as new modes of communication but as structural forces and pedagogical tools capable of expanding critical citizenship, animating public life, and extending democratic public spheres. While the cult of violence and culture of fear have become part of the visual reality dominating the spectacle of terrorism, it would be a mistake to simply align the new media exclusively with the forces of domination and commercialism, or what Alan Feldman calls "total-spectrum violence."[112]

What has to be stressed is the dialectical role of the new media within the larger political, social, and communicative landscape. It is too easy either to overly romanticize the new image-based technologies or to simply dismiss them as new sources of oppressive control. While the new media cannot be removed from the material relations of power and ideological effects of the spectacle of terrorism, it would be politically unproductive to associate the new media exclusively with the forces of domination and terror that are state-generated or mobilized by stateless forces. There is a certain political dreariness and undiluted pessimism that informs much of the left-oriented discourse on the new media, suggesting a kind of panoptical nightmare in which such media are viewed as more efficient technologies that expand the reach and scope of oppression and commodification. And yet, even within the spectacle of terrorism, there are hints of structural forces and elements of resistance that could be used for emancipatory rather than oppressive purposes. For instance, the spectacle of terrorism, with its recognition of the image as a key force of social power, makes clear that cultural politics is now constituted by a plurality of sites of resistance and social struggle, offering up new ways for progressives to conceptualize how the new media might be used to create alternative public spheres, as in, for instance, pirate radio, alternative film production, new interactive forms of communication, and so on. Theorists such as Mark Poster, Douglas Kellner, and Jacques Derrida are right in suggesting that the new electronic technologies and media publics "remove restrictions on the horizon of possible communications"[113] and, in doing so, suggest new possibilities for engaging the media as a democratic political and pedagogical force not merely for critique but for positive intervention and change.

Both the spectacle of the September 11th bombings and the beheading videos communicate far more than grisly acts of terror and atrocity. They also "point to ... a new structural feature of the international state system: that the historical monopoly of the means of destruction by the state is now at risk."[114] The spectacle of terrorism illustrates the degree to which state and corporate power can be challenged while suggesting the importance of what it means to address audiences through a political discourse whose aim is to defend democratic society at all costs. Such a defense points to a reclaiming of the social from the "necropolitics" of state-sanctioned and stateless terrorists.[115] Similarly, a democratic defense of the social also has to be waged on another front, currently dominated by a neoliberal discourse that pits market efficiency, privatization, profit, and capital accumulation against the redistribution of wealth, the funding of public services, substantive equality as a core political value, and the expansion of public ownership. At stake here is asking not only hard questions concerning how to imagine the basic elements of a social democracy but also what it would mean to expand the reach of democratic values and what can be commonly owned by recognizing that limits have to be placed on markets and the drive for profits regardless of the social costs. Equally important, a defense of common social goods, equality, redistribution of wealth, collective protection against risk, racial and economic justice, public ownership, and critical education has to take place at a time when democracy is being endlessly invoked as a justification for the culture of fear and, as such, is being symbolically emptied, suggesting a need to show how representations of democracy relate not just to matters of power, politics, and justice but also to security and fear.

Thomas Keenan is right to insist that "we cannot have a properly political relation to invasions and war crimes, military operations and paramilitary atrocities … in the present and future if we do not attend to the centrality of image product and management in them. We will be at an even greater loss if we do not admit that the high-speed electronic [image-based] media have created new opportunities not just for activism and awareness, but also for performance, presentation, advertising, propaganda, and for political work of all kinds."[116] The new media and screen culture are not the result of a simple merging of a new technology with the possibility for novel modes of cultural production; rather, they constitute a new stage in global capitalist development and must be grasped as structural phenomena that reconstitute the very terrain of the political. With the "global repositioning of visual communication practices, utilities, and techniques, ... the circulation of anthropologically threatening images of violence, terror, covert infection and social suffering has intensified in our public culture."[117] The new bio-politics linked to visual culture occupies an ever larger importance in global politics and must be further engaged as a key intervention into the realm of symbolic politics. The spectacle of terrorism, if examined closely, provides some resources for rethinking how the political is connected to particular understandings of the social; how distinctive modes of address are used to marshal specific identities, memories, and histories; and how certain pedagogical practices are employed to mobilize a range of affective investments around images of trauma and suffering. All of these issues raise important questions about how the new circuits of power, technology, and visual production rearticulate the relationships between meaning and action, modes of information and agency, affect and collectivity, and the public and the private.

Central to a rethinking of cultural politics is the issue of pedagogy both as a structural formation and as a moral and political practice. As a structural issue, the spectacle of terrorism illustrates that the power of the educational force of the culture, particularly in its use of image, sound, music, and visuality, has expanded to a range of new sites throughout the global public sphere. Pedagogy is now primarily public, no longer restricted to traditional sites of learning such as the school, family, or place of worship. Diverse material contexts and institutional forces, such as conservative foundations in the United States, fund new sites for the dissemination of knowledge, ranging from radio, cable, and television stations to high-speed Internet connections offering magazine and newspaper connections.[118] Think-tanks vie with pirate radio stations, alternative online zines, and blogs. Texts of numerous types now operate within global cultures of circulation, offering new discursive forms, modes of literacy, and types of interaction. The combination of new technologies and diverse modes of circulation is mediated, in turn, through various interpretative communities, which both situate texts and confer meanings in ways that cannot be specified in advance. Meanings are received, but they are not guaranteed, and posit an important terrain of struggle. And, while public pedagogy is the outgrowth of new public technologies,[119] the particular forms and ideologies it produces are almost always both the object of struggle and open to resistance.

What is crucial about the new sites of pedagogy is that they offer forms of pedagogical address that are often unique to the sites themselves and hence must be understood in terms of both the context that produces them and the spaces in which they are taken up. The concept of public pedagogy demands a radical rethinking of how visual and visualizing technologies are produced, circulated, and appropriated within diverse sites of pedagogy. Such sites generate forms of knowledge mediated through specific social relations and mobilize select ideologies, histories, and memories in response to particular problems. These diverse pedagogical sites also organize "personal and public structures of attention" and concern within specific circuits of power as part of their attempt to reach distinct audiences.[120] All of these contextual concerns bear heavily on what it would mean to understand these sites of pedagogy as important terrains of struggle in any viable notion of cultural politics. Crucial here are questions regarding what strategies are necessary to interpret, critically engage, and transform such sites as part of a broader struggle over the control of the new media and their use as a form of public pedagogy.

As a political and moral practice, critical pedagogies that seek to rupture the force of the spectacle need to foreground how the spectacle works to construct particular notions of agency and common sense, and how it would be possible to decouple the spectacularization of the image from the historical, political, economic, and social conditions through which it is constituted as an event. In part, this suggests analyzing the spectacle as part of a broader constellation of power by examining not only what forms of knowledge and agency it tries to put into place but also what is screened out and how the latter resonates with subordinate forms of critical knowledge and engagement. The spectacle of terrorism cannot work without a text, always involves issues of mediation, and borrows its forms (such as Reality TV?) from the larger culture; but at the same time, it attempts to close down any critical negotiation between brutality and rationality. All of these practices suggest modes of analysis that are not merely critical but pedagogical; that is, they involve learning how to deconstruct images, reading events within a related and broader context, and expanding the reach of critical reason to a range of texts and issues. Reading the new visual technologies requires not only critical skills but the ability to translate and negotiate their attempts to construct particular identities, flows of experience, and social events, past and future. In part, such tasks point to pedagogical practices that enable various audiences to recognize that digital, electronic, and computer-based technologies produce new ways of seeing that demand both new forms of literacy and new modes of intervention in determining how such technologies can be used democratically in governing our relationships to ourselves and others on a global scale. For instance, how might such image-based technologies be used to promote a public politics that enables viewers to recognize anti-democratic forms of power founded on substantive injustices and deep inequalities? How might such technologies be used to engage nature as part of the democratic commons, information as more than a commodity, knowledge as a social good, democracy as more than toothless elections, critical agency as an essential precondition for politics, space as a venue for nurturing critique and dialogue, and time as a necessary resource for meaningful citizenship?

Visualizing technologies and the events they produce not only deploy and are deployed by power; they are also intimately connected to the outgrowth of historical struggles over power, reinforcing the presupposition that such technologies cannot be separated from questions of control, inequality, access, justice, and politics. Roger Simon has suggested that there is a need for various cultural workers to develop pedagogical practices which encourage a form of attentiveness that enables audiences to engage in a dialogue with the stories told by spectacles of terrorism.[121] Such a pedagogy would reject the anti-intellectualism, the fear of critical dialogue, and the general indifference to the stories of others that are embedded in the pedagogy of the spectacle. Simon wants to challenge the way the spectacle privileges fear rather than persuasion and insists on the importance of pedagogical practices that undermine the highly individuated response solicited by the spectacle. It is imperative for audiences, in addressing what kind of pedagogical work is performed by the spectacle of terrorism, to analyze, first, how their own gaze might be aligned with the insidious modes and bodies of power that participate in images of destruction and, then, what is at stake in their attraction. The experience of the spectacle must be collectivized, addressed through pedagogical practices that assert its social articulations—that is, articulations of "remembering" how it mediates among different stories, contexts, and relations that privilege a public rather than a merely private sensibility. The spectacle of terrorism resonates with the entrenched spirit of social Darwinism, endemic to neoliberalism and the contemporary racial backlash, which powerfully undermines all notions of dialogue, critical engagement, and historical remembrance.[122] Instead of the latter, the spectacle of terrorism offers frozen thematic images of suffering, closes down the most elemental conditions necessary for democratic public spheres, and paralyzes critical agency through the privatization of a regressive notion of fear.

The spectacle of terrorism has no vision of the future outside of the culture of fear and the discourse of risk. Against such a pedagogy of closure, there is the need for a pedagogy that values a culture of questioning, views critical agency as a condition of public life, and rejects an intellectually paralyzing voyeurism in favor of the search for justice, which is inextricably linked to how we understand our relationship to others within a democratic global public sphere. Educators need to promote pedagogical practices based on the assumption that there is more hope in the world when teachers and students can question what is often taken for granted. For it is within the sphere of unlimited questioning and sustained dialogue that teachers and students can experience themselves as critical agents and learn how to oppose dogmatic forms of education that not only limit critical thinking but also undermine the capacity for self-determination, agency, self-representation, and effective democracy. By viewing the classroom and other pedagogical sites as a space of dialogue, critique, and translation, educators can offer a new language for imagining the mutual relationship between teaching and learning as both an act of critical understanding and competency and as the possibility of intervention—that is, to paraphrase Paulo Freire, learning to read the world critically in order to change it. Similarly, education must not be confused with training or merely educating students to be good technicians. Instead, education must address the development of both students' critical capacities and their ability to intervene in public life in ways that suggest that they know how to make public decisions and address the various ecological, economic, and social problems they confront on a local and global scale as well as know what it means to use education as a source of pleasure and joy. In this instance, pedagogy becomes meaningful and transformative to the degree to which it provides the knowledge, skills, and strategies that enable students to become responsible for their own ideas, to learn how to take risks, negotiate differences, be respectful of others, and think critically in order to function within a wider democratic culture. Such a pedagogy must reject the dystopian, anti-intellectual, and often racist vision at work in the spectacle of terrorism and, in doing so, provide a language of both criticism and hope as a condition for rethinking the possibilities of the future and the promise of global democracy itself.

Finally, any viable pedagogical struggle against the spectacle of terrorism must work diligently to rescue the social from the clutches of religious, market, and militaristic fundamentalists who have hijacked not only political institutions but a once-rich social imaginary, particularly in the United States over the last twenty years. The promise of a radical democracy must be articulated against the rabid discourse of neoliberal individualism, the utterly sectarian impulses of religious fundamentalists, neoconservative dreams of empire, and the authoritarian values of a newly energized militarism. Under the shadow of a growing authoritarianism, the spectacle of terrorism gives meaning to the social primarily through the modalities of xenophobia, violence, and death and, in doing so, makes fear the condition of unity, and the surrender of dissent and freedom the condition of agency. Image-based technologies have redefined the relationship between the ethical, political, and aesthetic. And while "the proximity is perhaps discomforting to some, ... it is also the condition of any serious intervention"[123] into what it means to connect cultural politics to matters of political and social responsibility. It is imperative that the social not be disconnected from the democratic possibilities of the new media and their rapidly expanding technologies. In part, this means rejecting the cynical positions put forth by theorists who believe that the new global media and virtual culture mark the terminal end of everything politically progressive, including the possibility of social criticism, collective struggle, critical agency, and any vestige of democracy.[124] Clearly, there is a need for progressives to rethink a notion of democracy that rejects the concept of passive citizenry, resurrects the concept of an expansive social contract, and refuses to decouple economic equality and difference from political democracy. Central to such a task is the resuscitation of public time in which matters of temporality become central to the experience of democracy—those conditions that enable participatory dialogue, open and informed debate, and a self-consciousness about what it means to learn, to question the very nature of learning, and to connect learning itself to social change. Democracy implies a certain kind of experience in which power is shared; dialogue is connected to involvement in the public sphere; competency is linked to intervention; and education enables a public capacity to deal with and respect differences that expand the range of values, capacities, and social forms that inform public life. Politics and pedagogy cannot be limited to matters of privatization, individualized fears, and insecurities—all to the exclusion of the public interest.

As the connection between public education and democracy is loosened, politics is devalued, and civic culture and public life deteriorate. The call for fundamental social transformation seems to be off the table as intellectuals appear both overwhelmed by the forces of domination and resigned to the growing forces of authoritarianism around the globe. Against this despair, intellectuals, educators, and others must provide a common ground for hope, one that acknowledges the power of social critique, new social movements, and the struggle for forms of democracy that extend beyond the boundaries of the nation-state. In this instance, pedagogy must work to enable students and others to think critically about the knowledge they gain, and how that knowledge is related to the power of self-definition, social responsibility, and collective struggle. Such a challenge also points to the necessity of providing the public with an expanded vision and a productive sense of the common good, a new language for what it means to translate private considerations into public concerns, and a deeply felt concern with how power can work in both the symbolic and material realms to produce vocabularies of critique and possibility in the service of a substantive and inclusive global democracy.

Toward an Oppositional Global Politics

Neoliberal globalization has not only destroyed the welfare state; it has privatized politics and, in doing so, offers only individualized (non)solutions to social problems. There is no public politics in neoliberal discourse—only the absolute private domain of competitive, self-interested individuals vying for their own ideological and material gain. Collective responsibility, like the concept of the public good, is either viewed as an antiquated discourse or dismissed as part of the pathology of a quaint, if not dangerous, liberalism. Any notion of the social that points to the necessity of both fostering a democratic global public sphere and rethinking critical citizenship is quickly emptied of any substance as it is collapsed into the imperatives of the marketplace and the ongoing "war against terrorism."

As the social is further undermined by the culture of fear, a corporatized media, and a growing authoritarianism in the United States and a number of other countries, it becomes all the more imperative for any viable challenge to the spectacle of terrorism to embrace those strategies and movements willing to raise "democracy and politics to the global level at which capital seeks and enjoys its freedom from human ideas of decency and justice."[125] This suggests that an oppositional global politics must get beyond the growing isolation of intellectuals from the activist movements that are developing across the globe. Such a politics needs a sober assessment of the growing democratic tendencies that are emerging in Latin America, particularly the opposition movements driving the center-left government in Argentina, the Workers' Party government in Brazil, and the anti-neoliberal government of Cesar Chavez in Venezuela. Any viable political analysis dealing with the spectacle must integrate a global perspective into its related discourses of critique, resistance, and social engagement.

Collective impotence results not only from abstracting freedom from the demands of the common good; it also results from a brutally expansive pedagogy of fear and cynicism that permeates all aspects of everyday culture. Global democracy faces a new challenge in a media-driven culture in which fear has become the most valuable currency of politics, and torture, exclusion, and murder its most effective consequences. A necessary part of the challenge ahead is to recognize that any viable democracy requires informed citizens with access to information that enables them to govern rather than simply be governed. Moreover, reclaiming the social as part of a broader democratic imaginary means drawing attention to the realities of power and authority and locating what Edward Said calls "the energy of resistance ... to all totalizing political movements and institutions and systems of thought"[126] across multiple and diverse spaces and borders. As Stanley Aronowitz points out, a new global politics cannot afford to ignore the new possibilities arising from the 1999 demonstrations by students and workers in Seattle as well as the "subsequent mass demonstrations at Quebec, Genoa and Spain against the key institutions of global capital, and the development of the World Social Forum, whose location in Brazil's Porto Alegre was symbolic of a global shift, as both an attempt to create a new civil society and a post-9/11 continuation of the protests."[127]

The spectacle of terrorism has developed a singular focus of communication and control, in part because of the atrophy of public discourse; but it is both too full and overburdened. Its excess and absences point to a collapse of politics and to an utterly restricted and debased notion of the social. The spectacle of terrorism may connect directly to the affairs of states through the new media, but any politics that matters will have to do more than engage the culture of the image and screen; it will also have to engage those material relations of power and institutions on local, national, and global levels that deploy information technologies. There is no going beyond the spectacle. Instead, the ideological, economic, pedagogical, and cultural conditions responsible for creating it have to be exposed and dismantled. Perhaps the central challenge here is to develop new forms of solidarity that not only address the conditions of authoritarianism and various fundamentalisms (such as neoliberal capitalism), responsible for a global culture of fear and insecurity, but also provide new ways of dealing with and defusing the felt experiences of fear, threat, and terrorism. What can be learned from the democratic relations that are being developed in places such as Northern Ireland, Israel, and Palestine, which are consistently being subjected to terrorism?[128] What is to be learned from the new South Africa as it mediates the legacy, torture, and abuses of apartheid through the forging of a new state, legal system, and set of social relations?[129] What is to be critically appropriated from oppositional cultures and their use of the new media as part of a large attempt to keep democracy alive? What might it mean to address the spectacle of terrorism as part of a broader attempt to make the pedagogical more political by developing social relations grounded in a sense of power, history, memory, justice, ethics, and hope, all of which would be seen as central to connecting the new media to global democratic struggles? Such a collective project requires a politics that is in the process of being invented, one that has to be attentive to the new realities of power, global social movements, neoliberal capitalism, and the promise of a planetary democracy.

Notes

1. Jean Baudrillard, "L'Espirit du Terrorisme," *South Atlantic Quarterly* 101, no. 2 (Spring 2002): 410.

2. Lewis H. Lapham, "Chasing the Pot," *Harper's Magazine* (July 2004), p. 11.

3. The relationship between the media and politics has been explored in far too many books to mention. Three different but useful texts are Robert McChesney, *The Problem of the Media* (New York: Monthly Review Press, 2004); Nick Couldry, *The Place of Media Power* (New York: Routledge, 2000); and Mark Poster, *The Second Media Age* (London: Polity Press, 1995). For a complex and brilliant analysis of the information society, see Scott Lash, *Critique of Information* (London: Sage, 2002). And for an excellent analysis of the relationship between politics and the importance of visual culture, see Nicholas Mirzoeff, *Watching Babylon: Global Visual Culture and the War in Iraq* (New York: Routledge, 2005).

4. Some important analyses of the relationship between the new media and aesthetics as well as critical commentaries on visual culture are Lev Manovich, *The Language of the New Media* (Cambridge, MA: MIT Press, 2001); Jessica Evans and Stuart Hall, eds., *Visual Culture: The Reader* (London: Sage, 1999); Hugh Mackay and Tim O' Sullivan, eds., *The Media Reader* (London: Sage, 1999); and Couldry, *The Place of Media Power*.

5. Classic work on the spectacle includes Guy Debord, *The Society of the Spectacle*, trans. Donald Nicholson-Smith (New York: Zone Books, 1967, reprinted in 1994); Jean Baudrillard, *Simulacra and Simulation* (Ann Arbor: University of Michigan Press, 1995); Douglas Kellner, *The Persian Gulf TV War* (Boulder, CO: Westview Press, 1992); Carol Becker, *Surpassing the Spectacle* (Boulder, CO: Rowman and Littlefield, 2002); Jean Baudrillard, *The Spirit of Terrorism*, trans. Chris Turner (London: Verso Press, 2002); Slavoj Zizek, *Welcome to the Desert of the Real* (London: Verso Press, 2002); Douglas Kellner, *Media Spectacle and the Crisis of Democracy* (Boulder, CO: Paradigm Press, 2005); and Retort (Iain Boal, T. J. Clark, Joseph Matthews, and Michael Watts), *Afflicted*

Powers: Capital and Spectacle in a New Age of War (London: Verso Press, 2005).

6. Eugene L. Arva, "Life as Show Time: Aesthetic Images and Ideological Spectacles," *Perspectives on Evil and Human Wickedness* 1, no. 2 (2003): 74.

7. For an important and complex understanding of the link between aesthetics and politics, especially fascism, see Lutz Koepnick, *Walter Benjamin and the Aesthetics of Power* (Lincoln: University of Nebraska Press, 1999). For a discussion of the fascist organization of leisure, see Victoria de Grazia, *The Culture of Consent* (London: Cambridge University Press, 1981). See also Michael Hardt and Antonio Negri, *Multitude: War and Democracy in the Age of Empire* (New York: Penguin Press, 2004). Hardt and Negri are entirely correct in arguing that under the Bush administration, "war has become the matrix for all relations of power" (p. 13).

8. President George W. Bush, "President Welcomes President Chirac to the White House," *White House News Release*, November 6, 2001, available online at http://www.whitehouse.gov/news/releases/2001/11/print/20011106-4.html.

9. Adnan R. Kahn, "Piety and Profits," *MacLeans.ca*, December 27, 2004, available online at http://www.macleans.ca/topstories/religion/article.jsp?content=20041227_96020_96020.

10. Brian Massumi, "Preface," in *The Politics of Everyday Fear*, ed. Brian Massumi (Minneapolis: University of Minnesota Press, 1993), p. viii.

11. These themes are brilliantly explored in Jean and John Comaroff, "Criminal Obsessions, After Foucault: Postcoloniality, Policing, and the Metaphysics of Disorder," *Critical Inquiry* 30 (Summer 2004), pp. 800–824, and Achille Mbembe, "Necropolitics" (trans. Libby Meintje), *Public Culture* 15, no. 1 (2003), pp. 11–40.

12. Retort (Iain Boal, T. J. Clark, Joseph Matthews, and Michael Watts,), "Afflicted Powers: The State, the Spectacle, and September 11," *New Left Review* 27 (May–June 2004): 16.

13. Marina Warner, "Disembodied Eyes, or the Culture of Apocalypse," *Open Democracy*, April 18, 2005, pp. 1–2, available online at www.OpenDemocracy.net.

14. Ibid. For instance, Steven Bochko's thirteen-episode television series "Over There" is being aired as one of the "first American television series that has tried to process a war as entertainment while it was still being fought." Billed as a program "that dramatizes wartime slaughter and suffering, with its expertly filmed battle scenes . . . limbs torn off by exploding mines," the series reproduces a central assumption of the spectacle of terrorism: that politics is war, and violence is its most important commodity. See Alessandra Stanley, "The Drama of Iraq, While It Still Rages," *New York Times*, July 27, 2005, available online at http://www.nytimes.com/2005/07/27/arts/television/27stan.html?8hpib.

15. This idea comes from Mbembe, "Necropolitics."

16. Debord, *Society of the Spectacle*; Kellner, *Persian Gulf TV War*; Kellner, *Media Spectacle and the Crisis of Democracy* (Boulder, CO: Paradigm Press, 2005).

17. Steve Best and Douglas Kellner, "Debord, Cybersituations, and the Interactive Spectacle," *Illuminations*, December 26, 2004, pp. 1–16, available online at http://www.uta.edu/huma/illuminations/best6.htm.

18. Candace Vogler and Patchen Markell, "Introduction: Violence, Redemption, and the Liberal Imagination," *Public Culture* 15, no. 1 (Winter 2003): 1.

19. See Roger I. Simon, Mario DiPaolantoni, and Mark Clamen, "Remembrance as Praxis and the Ethics of the Inter Human," *Culture Machine*, October 24, 2004, pp. 1–33, available online at http://culturemachine.tees.ac.uk/Cmach/Backissues/j1004/Articles/simon.htm.

20. I am in agreement with John and Jean Comaroff, who argue that the obsession with crime and violence is increasingly becoming central to the definition of the nation-state (though the authors are referring to South Africa) and that

the "theatricality of premodern power" has complicated the internalized, capillary kinds of discipline described by Foucault. Power now has a face, visible in its brute show of force, strength, policing, militarizing, and surveillance. See Jean and John Comaroff, "Criminal Obsessions, After Foucault: Postcoloniality, Policing, and the Metaphysics of Disorder," *Critical Inquiry* 30 (Summer 2004): 804.

21. Mbembe, "Necropolitics," pp. 11–12.

22. Ibid., pp. 17, 23.

23. Jean Baudrillard, "L'Espirit du Terrorisme," *South Atlantic Quarterly* 101, no. 2 (Spring 2002): 413.

24. The return to "the real," as used here, is not unlike Slavoj Žižek's claim that what was once experienced as a kind of spectral fantasy by Americans, whether the spectacle of Third World disasters or the apocalyptic horrors virtualized in Hollywood films, has now intruded into reality. See Žižek, *Welcome to the Desert of the Real.*

25. Two qualifications need to be made here. First, I am not suggesting that there is a clean break with the past and the politics of consumerism. Second, my point is not that fear and terrorism have replaced consumerism but, rather, that they have added to it in a way that creates a new kind of fear, one that is not merely an extension of the logic of consumerism.

26. I am not suggesting here that image-based culture is on the side of authoritarianism and that print culture is on the side of debate and literacy, as some theorists have claimed. Rather, I am arguing that there are different modalities of literacies operating in complex ways in different historical formations and that, at present, the modality of address organized through aural and image-based culture constitutes a new set of linkages among the culture of fear, the politics of terrorism, and image-based culture.

27. Lutz Koepnick, "Aesthetic Politics Today: Walter Benjamin and Post-Fordist Culture," in *Critical Theory: Current State and Future Prospects,* ed. Peter Uwe Hohendahl

and Jaimey Fisher (New York: Berghahn Books, 2001), pp. 95–96.

28. Susan Sontag, "Fascinating Fascism," *New York Review of Books*, February 6, 1975, available online at http://www.history.ucsb.edu/faculty/marcuse/classes/33d/33dTexts/SontagFascinFascism75.htm.

29. Allen Feldman, "On the Actuarial Gaze: From 9/11 to Abu Ghraib," *Cultural Studies* 19, no. 2 (March 2005): 215.

30. Paul Gilroy, *Against Race* (Cambridge, MA: Harvard University Press, 2000), p. 146.

31. Koepnick, "Aesthetic Politics," p. 96.

32. Ibid., p. 95.

33. Rey Chow, "Fascist Longings in Our Midst," *Ariel* 26, no. 1 (January 1995): 38.

34. Gilroy, *Against Race*, p. 150.

35. Ibid., p. 159.

36. Cited in Retort, "Afflicted Powers," p. 8. The publication information for Debord's *The Society of the Spectacle* can be found in Note 5.

37. Debord, *Society of the Spectacle*, p. 19.

38. Ibid., p. 12.

39. Ibid., p. 13.

40. Ibid., p. 12.

41. Ibid., p. 14.

42. Ibid., p. 14; original emphasis.

43. Ibid., p. 24.

44. Retort, "Afflicted Powers," p. 9.

45. Ibid., p. 8.

46. Debord, *Society of the Spectacle*, p. 18.

47. Arva, "Life as Show Time," p. 70.

48. Debord, *Society of the Spectacle*, p. 30.

49. Arva, "Life as Show Time," p. 76.

50. Koepnick, "Aesthetic Politics," p. 108.

51. See Lash, *Critique of Information.*

52. Mark Poster, *The Information Subject* (Amsterdam: Gordon and Breach, 2001), p. 127.

53. For a brilliant exploration of the new information technologies and their connection to war, terror, and new resistance movements, see Chris Hables Gray, *Peace, War, and Computers* (New York: Routledge, 2005). On the importance of the networked society giving rise to new forms of resistance, see Hardt and Negri, *Multitude*.

54. Stanley Aronowitz, *Dead Artists, Live Theories, and Other Cultural Problems* (New York: Routledge, 1994), p. 42.

55. James Castonguay, "Conglomeration, New Media, and the Cultural Production of the 'War on Terror,'" *Cinema Journal* 43, no. 4 (Summer 2004): 106.

56. Koepnick, "Aesthetic Politics," p. 95.

57. This issue is analyzed in detail in Corey Robin, *Fear: The History of a Political Idea* (New York: Oxford University Press, 2004).

58. I have taken up these issues in more detail in Henry A. Giroux, *Public Spaces/Private Lives: Democracy Beyond 9/11* (Boulder, CO: Rowman and Littlefield, 2003); *The Abandoned Generation: Democracy Beyond the Culture of Fear* (New York: Palgrave, 2004); and *The Terror of Neoliberalism: The New Authoritarianism and the Eclipse of Democracy* (Boulder, CO: Paradigm Press, 2004).

59. Giorgio Agamben, "On Security and Terror," trans. Soenke Zehle, *Frankfurter Allgemeine Zeitung*, September 20, 2001, available online at http://egs.edu/faculty/agamben/agamben-on-security-and-terror.html.

60. This idea comes from a personal correspondence with John Comaroff dated August 9, 2005.

61. Stanley Aronowitz, "The Retreat to Postmodern Politics," *Situations* 1, no. 1 (April 2005): 32.

62. Giorgio Agamben touches on the relationship between the culture of fear and the state of emergency in his comment that "President Bush's decision to refer to himself constantly

as the 'Commander in Chief of the Army' after September 11, 2001 must be considered in the context of this presidential claim to sovereign powers in emergency situations. If, as we have seen, the assumption of this title entails a direct reference to the state of exception, then Bush is attempting to produce a situation in which the emergency becomes the rule, and the very distinction between peace and war (and between foreign and civil war) becomes impossible." See Agamben, *State of Exception* (Chicago: University of Chicago Press, 2005), p. 23.

63. Francois Debrix, "Cyberterror and Media-Induced Fears: The Production of Emergency Culture," *Strategies* 14, no. 1 (2001): 152.

64. Of course, there is the related work of Jean Baudrillard, Slavoj Žižek, and Thomas Keenan; but rather than taking up these authors separately, I have tried to incorporate their ideas about how the new regime of the spectacle moves the issue of struggle into the realm of the symbolic. See Baudrillard, *Spirit of Terrorism;* Žižek, *Welcome to the Desert of the Real;* and Keenan, "Mobilizing Shame," *South Atlantic Quarterly* 103, no. 2/3 (2004): 435–449.

65. Kellner's most recent book on the subject is *Media Spectacle and the Crisis of Democracy* (Boulder, CO: Paradigm Press, 2005).

66. Best and Kellner, "Debord, Cybersituations," p. 3.

67. On the spectacle and schooling, see Kevin D. Vinson and E. Wayne Ross, "The Power of High-Stakes Testing," in *Education as Enforcement,* ed. Kenneth J. Saltman and David A. Gabbard (New York: Routledge, 2003), pp. 241–258.

68. Kellner takes up both of these wars as part of his theory of the spectacle in *Persian Gulf TV War* and *Media Spectacle and the Crisis of Democracy.*

69. Douglas Kellner, "Media Culture and the Triumph of the Spectacle," *Razon Y Palabra* 39 (April–May 2004): 13.

70. Ibid., p. 13.

71. Retort, "Afflicted Powers," p. 13.

72. I want to thank Susan Searls Giroux for this idea and for pointing me to Achille Mbembe's work, which explores the issue of state violence being endemic to modernity and state rule. The cited quote can be found on page 18 of Mbembe's "Necropolitics."

73. Eric L. Santer, "Some Reflections on States of Exception," in *Social Insecurity,* ed. Len Guenther and Cornelius Hesters (Toronto: Anansi Press, 2000), p. 157.

74. Gary R. Bunt, *Islam in the Digital Age: E-Jihad, Online Fatwas, and Cyber Islamic Environments* (London: Pluto Press, 2003).

75. The beheading videos certainly have had the most impact in forcing the hand of various governments to deal directly or indirectly with the terrorists. In Baghdad, the popularity of porno discs has been replaced by that of beheading videos. See J. M. Berger, "New Terror Tactic: Sidewalk Beheadings Hit Iraq," *Intelwire.com,* January 21, 2005, available online at http://intelwire.egoplex.com/; Patrick J. McDonnell, "Confession Videos Transfix Iraqis," *Los Angeles Times,* March 2, 2005, available online at www.freenewmexican.com; Matthew McAllester, "Iraqi Beheadings Now Fueling Global 'Snuff' Film Market," *Star Tribune,* October 17, 2004, available online at http://virtuallyislamic.blogspot.com/2004_10_01_virtuallyislamic_archive.html; Hamza Hendawi, "Horror Stars on Iraqi TV Screens: Videos of Beheadings Replace Porn as Fare," *Messinger-Inquirer.com,* September 27, 2004, available online at http://www.Messinger-Inquirer.com; and News Wire Services, "Death Videos Big Sellers," *New York Daily News,* September 27, 2004, available online at http://www.nydailynews.com/front/story/236229p-202702c.html.

76. Ibrahim al-Marashi, "Iraq's Hostage Crisis: Kidnappings, Mass Media in the Iraqi Insurgency," *Middle East Review of International Affairs* 8, no. 4 (December 2004): 8.

77. Hendawi, "Horror Stars on Iraqi TV Screens," p. 1.

78. Ibid.

79. al-Marashi, "Iraq's Hostage Crisis," p. 12.

80. ABC News, "Video of Beheadings Found for Sale at Tampa Gas Station," *ABC Action News*, November 9, 2004, available online at http://www.wfts.com/stories/2004/11/041109videos.html.

81. McAllester, "Iraqi Beheadings."

82. Cited in ibid.

83. Sinan Salaheddin, "Iraq Beheadings: Medium Becomes Message," *ABC 7 News*, September 23, 2004, available online at http://www.wjla.com/headlines/0904/175208.html.

84. Hardt and Negri, *Multitude*, p. 332.

85. For a brilliant analysis of the role of the new media and the realm of the virtual, see Poster, *Information Subject*, and Nick Couldry, *Contesting Media Power: Alternative Media in a Networked World* (Boulder, CO: Rowman and Littlefield, 2003).

86. Paul Marshall, "War Against the Infidels the Message Behind the Beheadings," *Weekly Standard*, July 5, 2004, available online at http://www.freedomhouse.org/religion/country/Saudi%20Arabia/War%20Against%20the%20Infidels.htm?article_id=170.

87. Ted Koppel, "Nightline: Images of War," *ABCNewsStore.com*, September 23, 2003, available online at http://www.ABCNEWSstore.com.

88. Neal Gabler, "Downloading Death," *Salon.com*, May 13, 2004, available online at http://www.salon.com/ent/feature/2004/05/13/berg/print.html.

89. Of course, Ignatieff is a liberal whom the conservatives love since he believes that torture can be discussed in reasonable ways and that the might of empire can be defended as long as it makes a claim to democracy. For an insightful critique of Ignatieff's politics, see Mariano Aguirre, "Exporting Democracy, Revising Torture: The Complex Missions of Michael Ignatieff," *Open Democracy*, July 15, 2005, available online at www.OpenDemocracy.net.

90. Michael Ignatieff, "The Terrorist as Auteur," *New York Times Magazine*, November 14, 2004, p. 50.

91. Ibid., pp. 52–53.

92. See the "Iraqi Body Count Press Release," *Iraq Body Count Project*, July 19, 2005, available online at http://www.iraqbodycount.net/press/pr12.php.

93. Although important critiques holding great promise emerged in the aftermath of the events of 9/11, these have rarely been applied to the more general spectacle of terrorism. See, for example, Jonathan Flatley, "All That Is Solid Melts into Air: Notes on the Logic of the Global Spectacle," *Afterimage* 30, no. 2 (September/October 2002): 4–5; Samuel Weber, "War, Terrorism, and Spectacle: On Towers and Caves," *South Atlantic Quarterly* 10, no. 3 (Summer 2002): 449–458; Jean Baudrillard, "L'Espirit du Terrorisme," *South Atlantic Quarterly* 101, no. 2 (Spring 2002): 403–415; Arva, "Life as Show Time"; Douglas Kellner, "September 11, Spectacles of Terror, and Media Manipulation: A Critique of Jihadist and Bush Media Politics," *Logos* 2, no. 1 (Winter 2003): 86–102, available online at http://www.gseis.ucla.edu/faculty/keener/ed270/index.html; and Allen Feldman, "On the Actuarial Gaze: From 9/11 to Abu Ghraib," *Cultural Studies* 19, no. 2 (March 2005): 203–226.

94. Patrick J. McDonnell, "Confession Videos Transfix Iraqis," *Associated Press*, March 2, 2005, available online at http://www.freenewmexican.com.

95. Ibid.

96. Ibid.

97. Gary Gately, "Police Counter Dealers' DVD with One of Own," *New York Times*, May 11, 2005, p. A12.

98. BBC News, "Serbian Leader 'Shocked' by Video," June 19, 2005, available online at http://news.bbc.co.uk/1/hi/world/europe/4605223.stm.

99. I want to thank my long-time friend Roger Simon for the ideas that frame this section on memory and the workings of the spectacle.

100. Davin Allen Grindstaff and Kevin Michael DeLuca, "The Corpus of Daniel Pearl," *Critical Studies in Media Communication* 21, no. 4 (December 2004): 310. Grindstaff and

DeLuca provide an extensive and insightful analysis of how the Pearl video has been transformed into raw material for multiple discourses about terrorism, nationalism, and memory.

101. On the influence of militarism in the United States, see Andrew J. Bacevich, *The New American Militarism* (New York: Oxford University Press, 2004).

102. Ibid., p. 2.

103. Agamben, "On Security and Terror."

104. Feldman, "On the Actuarial Gaze," p. 207.

105. See Naomi Klein, *No Logo: No Space, No Choice, No Jobs* (New York: Picador, 2002).

106. I take up this issue in Henry A. Giroux, *Against the New Authoritarianism* (Winnipeg: Arbeiter Ring Publishing, 2005).

107. This idea comes from Jean and John Comaroff, "Criminal Obsessions," p. 819.

108. Retort, "Afflicted Powers," p. 15.

109. Mary Kaldor, "How to Free Hostages: War, Negotiation, or Law-enforcement," *Open Democracy*, September 19, 2004, available online at http://www.OpenDemocracy.net. This is a position also taken up in detail and with great force by Hardt and Negri, *Multitude*.

110. Jacques Derrida cited in Michael Peters, "The Promise of Politics and Pedagogy in Derrida," *Review of Education/Pedagogy/Cultural Studies* (in press).

111. Poster, *The Information Subject*, pp. 132–133.

112. Feldman, "On the Actuarial Gaze," p. 212.

113. Jürgen Habermas, *Theory of Communicative Action, Vol. 2. Lifeworld and System: A Critique of Functionalist Reason*, trans. Thomas McCarthy (Cambridge, UK: Polity Press, 1987), p. 390.

114. Retort, "Afflicted Powers," p. 17.

115. The concept of necropolitics is taken from Mbembe, "Necropolitics."

116. Keenan, "Mobilizing Shame," pp. 441–442.

117. Feldman, "On the Actuarial Gaze," p. 203.

118. Lewis H. Lapham, "Tentacles of Rage—The Republican Propaganda Mill, A Brief History," *Harper's Magazine*, September 2004, pp. 31–41.

119. Dilip Parameshwar Gaonkar and Elizabeth A. Povinelli, "Technologies of Public Forms: Circulation, Transfiguration, Recognition," *Public Culture* 15, no. 3 (2003): 385–397.

120. Sharon Sliwinski, "A Painful Labour: Responsibility and Photography," *Visual Studies* 19, no. 2 (2004): 148.

121. See Roger I. Simon, Mario DiPaolantoni, and Mark Clamen, "Remembrance as Praxis and the Ethics of the Inter Human," *Culture Machine*, October 24, 2004, pp. 1–33, available online at http://culturemachine.tees.ac.uk/Cmach/Backissues/j1004/Articles/simon.htm.

122. Some excellent sources on neoliberalism are Pierre Bourdieu, *Acts of Resistance* (New York: Free Press, 1989); Noam Chomsky, *Profit over People: Neoliberalism and the Global Order* (New York: Seven Stories Press, 1999); Zygmunt Bauman, *The Individualized Society* (London: Polity Press, 2001); Colin Leys, *Market Driven Politics* (London: Verso, 2001); Jean and John Comaroff, eds., *Millennial Capitalism and the Culture of Neoliberalism* (Chicago: University of Chicago Press, 2001); Doug Henwood, *After the New Economy* (New York: The New Press, 2003); Kevin Phillips, *Wealth and Democracy: A Political History of the American Rich* (New York: Broadway, 2003); Paul Krugman, *The Great Unraveling: Losing Our Way in the New Century* (New York: W. W. Norton, 2003; David Harvey, *The New Imperialism* (New York: Oxford University Press, 2003); William Greider, "The Right's Grand Ambition: Rolling Back the 20th Century," *The Nation*, May 12, 2003, pp. 1–12; Lisa Duggan, *The Twilight of Equality: Neoliberalism, Cultural Politics, and the Attack on Democracy* (Boston: Beacon Press, 2003); Henry A. Giroux, *The Terror of Neoliberalism* (Boulder: Paradigm Publishers, 2004); and Neil Smith, *The Endgame of Globalization* (New York: Routledge, 2005).

123. Keenan, "Mobilizing Shame," p. 447. Keenan explores the relationship between ethics and responsibility in even greater detail in his *Fables of Responsibility* (Stanford: Stanford University Press, 1997).

124. See, for instance, Jean Baudrillard, *Spirit of Terrorism*. We also find a disquieting element of this political despair in Feldman, "On the Actuarial Gaze," pp. 203–226, and Retort, "Afflicted Powers," pp. 5–21.

125. Daniel Leighton, "Searching for Politics in an Uncertain World: Interview with Zygmunt Bauman," *Renewal: A Journal of Labour Politics* 10, no. 1 (Winter 2002): 14.

126. Edward W. Said, *Power, Politics, and Culture: Interviews with Edward W. Said*, ed. Gauri Viswanathan (New York: Vintage Books, 2001), p. 65.

127. Stanley Aronowitz, "The Retreat to Postmodern Politics," *Situations* 1, no. 1 (April 2005): 43.

128. I want to thank Roger Simon for this suggestion.

129. Some of the most important work on South Africa and postcolonialism can be found in various essays by John and Jean Comaroff. See, for example, John L. Comaroff and Jean Comaroff, "Nurturing the Nation: Aliens, Apocalypse and the Post Colonial State," *Journal of South African Studies* 27, no. 3 (September 2001): 627–651; John L. Comaroff and Jean Comaroff, *Cultural Policing in Postcolonial South Africa* (Chicago: American Bar Federation, 1999); John L. Comaroff and Jean Comaroff, "Reflections on the Colonial State, in South Africa and Elsewhere: Factions, Fragments, Facts and Fictions," *Social Identities* 4, no. 3 (October 1998): 321–361; and John L. Comaroff and Jean Comaroff, eds., *Civil Society and Political Imagination in South Africa* (Chicago: University of Chicago Press, 1999).

◇

Index

abstraction, linguistic, 7–8

abstract principles, 25

Abu Ghraib prison, 50, 51

Agamben, Giorgio, 42, 64, 89–90n. 62

agency, 14, 23, 25, 37; decline of, 6–7, 62, 77–79; fascist spectacle and, 32–33; resistance and, 39–41, 68, 74–75

anti-Semitism, 61

Aronowitz, Stanley, 41, 43, 82

Arva, Eugene L., 38

authoritarianism, 1, 6–7, 78; democracy transformed into, 66, 67; legitimation of, 42–43, 63–64; rise of, 7–8

Bacevich, Andrew J., 9

Badiou, Alain, 5

Baudrillard, Jean, 19, 65

Bauman, Zygmunt, 5

beheading videos, 13, 25–27, 50–56, 65, 70; commentary on, 55–56, 93n. 99; Pearl video, 61, 93n. 99; sales of, 52–54, 91n. 75

Berg, Nicholas, 53

binarisms, 64–65

bloggers, 40–41

Bocho, Steven, 86n. 14

Brazil, 81, 82

Bunt, Gary, 51

Buried in the Sand, 53

Bush, George W., 9, 21–22, 24, 25, 89–90

Bush administration, 8

cable news, 21

camera, as instrument of terror, 56–57

capitalism, 6, 22; spectacle and, 28–29, 34–38, 44, 46, 48–49

carceral state, 64, 66

Castonguay, James, 41

Chavez, Cesar, 81

citizenship, 1–3, 30, 63

civilization vs. barbarism, discourse of, 24–25

closure, pedagogy of, 76–77

collective responsibility, 1, 80–81

Comaroff, Jean, 86n. 20, 96n. 128

Comaroff, John, 42, 86n. 20, 96n. 128

compassion, neutralization of, 12, 49

consensus, built around fear, 49–50, 65

conservative foundations, 73

consumerism, 1–3, 64, 87n. 25; spectacle of terrorism and, 30–31, 34–36, 87n. 25

cultural politics, 14–16, 35, 70; reclaiming of democracy, 68–69; sites of pedagogy, 73–74; spectacle and, 27–28, 36–37

culture of fear, 1–3, 6–7, 11–12, 86n. 20

Debord, Guy, 27, 34–39, 44, 46, 47, 49

Debrix, Francois, 44

democracy, 66–67; collective vision, 5–6; reclaiming, 68–71

domination, mediated by images, 36–38

drug dealers, videos produced by, 59

economic uncertainty, 22, 23

education, 10–11, 77–78

emergency, state of, 43–44, 89–90n. 62

ethics, reduction of, 2–3, 6, 7, 33, 46, 57

everyday life, colonization of, 36–37

fantasy, 4, 11, 27, 38, 64, 87n. 24

fascism, 29, 32–34

fear, 64–65, 71; culture of, 1–3,

6–7, 11–12, 86n. 20; individualization of, 24, 31, 67, 76–77; postmodern, 43–44; sense of unity and, 2, 29–30, 33; social consensus built around, 49–50, 65
Federal Bureau of Investigation, 10–11
Feldman, Allen, 32, 69
Foucault, Michel, 49
Frankfurt School, 36, 38
Freire, Paulo, 77

Gabler, Neal, 56
ghost sociability, 23
giganticism, 32
Gilroy, Paul, 34
globalization, 3–4, 15, 39–40
global justice movements, 40–41, 82
global politics, 72, 81–82
Gonzalez, Alberto, 2
good and evil, discourse of, 21–22, 64–65
Gramsci, Antonio, 36

Hendawi, Hamza, 52

Holocaust, 7, 61
homelessness, 4–5
hope, 16, 77, 78
Hurricane Katrina, 4
Hussein, Saddam, 53
hyper-real displays of violence, 11–12, 24, 25, 31. *See also* Reality TV

Ignatieff, Michael, 56–58, 92n. 88
image-based media, 3–5, 26, 31, 87n. 26; camera as instrument of terror, 56–57; dialectical role of, 69–70; globalization and, 39–40, 72; insurgent-produced videos, 49–55, 66; resistance and, 52, 67–72; screen culture, 2, 20, 34. *See also* media; spectacle of terrorism; technologies, visual
images: domination mediated by, 36–38; globalization and, 39–40; war of, 65–66
individualism, 1, 4, 78, 80

individualization of fear,
24, 31, 67, 76–77
insurgent-produced
videos, 49–55, 66
interactive spectacle,
45–46
Internet, 21, 41, 51, 53–54
Iraq, U.S. occupation of,
46, 57–58. *See also*
videos

justice, war against, 65

Kaldor, Mary, 67
Keenan, Thomas, 71–72
Keep Talking, 59
Kellner, Douglas, 27,
44–47
Klinker, Dan, 54
Koepnick, Lutz, 39
Koppel, Ted, 56

Laden, Osama bin, 21–22
Lapham, Lewis H., 19
Latin America, 81
lawlessness, 7, 16, 23,
30, 67
left-oriented discourse,
14, 70, 79

legitimation, 1, 42–43,
63–64
literacy, modes of, 73, 75,
87n. 26

Macdonald, Dwight, 7
Marashi, Ibrahim al-, 52,
53
Marshall, Paul, 56
Marxism, 36
Massumi, Brian, 22
McAllester, Matthew,
53–54
McDonald's spectacle, 46
media, 7, 11; centrality
of, 19–20; civilization
vs. barbarism,
discourse of, 24–25;
critical engagement
of, 14–16; investment
in spectacularizing
violence and fear,
7–8, 10; promotion of
sense of vulnerability,
63–64; ratings, 52;
second age of, 40–42;
as technology for
redefining politics, 12–
13. *See also* beheading
videos; image-based
media

megaspectacle, 45
memory, 11, 60–63, 76
militarism, 1, 8–10, 63
Monbiot, George, 10

National Security Higher
  Education Advisory
  Board, 10–11
necropolitics, 71, 94n.
  114
neoliberalism, 2, 6, 22,
  43, 71, 83
new media. *See* image-
  based media
Nightline, 56
Nike spectacle, 46

O. J. Simpson trial, 45
"Over There," 86n. 14

Pearl, Daniel, 61, 93n. 99
pedagogy: of closure,
  76–77; as moral and
  political practice, 72,
  74; of questioning,
  77–78; as structural
  formation, 72–74. *See
  also* public pedagogy
permanent war, 8, 20, 43,
  63, 68

Persian Gulf TV War, 46
police brutality, 59–60
political spectacle, 46, 47
politics: culture as site of,
  14–16; global, 72, 81–
  82; media as technology
  for redefining, 12–13;
  necropolitics, 71, 94n.
  114; neutralization
  of, 31, 42; pedagogy
  as practice of, 72, 74;
  privatization of, 80;
  violence, relationship
  with, 20–23, 48, 67; as
  warlike relation, 48
Pollock, Grace, 4
possibility, 5
Poster, Mark, 40
postmodern fear, 43–44
poverty, 4
power relations, 14
privatization, capitalistic,
  43, 62
privatization of politics,
  1–6, 8, 76–77, 79–80
public, collapsed into
  private, 1–4
public pedagogy, 5, 38,
  47; of fear, 65–66;
  function of spectacle, 2,
  12–14, 22, 24, 27–28,
  36–37; redefinition of,

26–27; sites of, 14–16, 58, 73–74. *See also* pedagogy

questioning, pedagogy of, 77–78

racism, 4, 29
radical politics, culture as site of, 14–16
Reality TV, 3–4, 7, 58–59
religious fundamentalism, 48, 66
resistance: agency and, 39–41, 68, 74–75; dialectical role of new media, 69–70; image-based media and, 52, 67–72; pedagogy as moral and political practice, 72, 74; pedagogy as structural formation, 72–74; plurality of sites of, 14–16, 70; questions about new media, 67–68; rethinking democracy, 68–69; structural features of state system, 70–71. *See also* spectacle of terrorism

responsibility, collective, 1, 80–81
right to kill, 30
Rodney King video, 59–60
Rumsfeld, Donald, 6

Said, Edward, 82
Salaheddin, Sinan, 54–55
screen culture, 2, 20, 34
Seattle protests, 41, 82
second media age, 40–42
security state. See state
September 11th, 2001 terrorist attacks, 8, 23–24, 44; visual imagery of, 47, 50, 55, 62
Serbian video, 60
shock and awe, 8, 13, 21, 24, 30, 46, 55
Simon, Roger, 76
social imaginary, 78
social movements, 40–41
society of the spectacle, 37–38, 49
Society of the Spectacle, The (Debord), 34–39, 44, 46, 47, 49
space, 39–40
Spanier, Graham, 11

spectacle: capitalism and, 28–29, 34–38, 44, 46, 48–49; changing nature of, 26, 44–49; consent and, 28–30; consumerism and, 30–31, 34–36, 87n. 25; cultural politics and, 27–28, 36–37; fascist, 32–34; history of, 27–28; interactive, 45–46; internal contradictions, 46–47; megaspectacle, 45; pedagogical function of, 2, 12–14, 22, 24, 27–28, 36–37; political, 46, 47; reemergence of older forms of control, 49, 54–55; screen culture, 2, 20, 34; terrorism as, 1–2, 8, 10, 47; unity, sense of, 2, 29–30, 33

spectacle of terrorism, 22, 30–31, 42, 44, 47–48; cultural memories and, 60–63; emotional truth of, 60–61; insurgent-produced videos, 49–55, 66; legitimation of authoritarianism,

63–64; media ratings and, 52; movie sales of beheadings, 52–54, 91n. 75; plurality of sites of resistance, 70; political effects of, 57–58; text of, 74–75. *See also* beheading videos; image-based media; resistance; terror of the spectacle

sports spectacle, 46
Srebrenica massacre, 60
state, 10, 13; carceral, 64, 66; legitimation of authoritarianism, 42–43; structural features of, 70–71; terrorism, 48, 51
state of emergency, 43–44, 89–90n. 62
Stop Snitching, 59

Tadic, Boris, 60
talk radio, 55
technologies, visual, 31, 35, 87n. 26; development of spectacle and, 44–45; fascist spectacle and, 32–34; renewal of

democracy and, 68–69; resistance and, 52, 68–70. See also image-based media; videos
temporality, 39–40, 79
terrorism: as spectacle, 1–2, 8, 10, 47; visual theater of, 21. See also war on terrorism
Terrorism in the Grip of Justice, 58
terror of the spectacle, 26, 28–31, 64. See also spectacle of terrorism
texts, 73–75
total-spectrum violence, 69

unity, sense of, 2, 29–30, 33

Venezuela, 81
videos: government-sponsored, 58–59; insurgent-produced, 49–55, 66; of kidnapped hostages, 51, 52; police productions, 59; Rodney King, 59–60. *See also* beheading videos

violence: discourse of good and evil, 21–22; hyper-real displays of, 11–12, 24, 25, 31; politics, relationship with, 20–23, 48, 67; as strategy of representation, 25–26
visual symbolism, 7–8

war, permanent, 8, 20, 43, 63, 68
Warner, Marina, 23
war of images, 65–66
war on terrorism, 2–3, 8, 12–13, 65; discourse of good and evil, 21–22; as megaspectacle, 45; reorganization of domestic public space, 8–10; second media age and, 41–42; state of emergency and, 43
Workers' Party (Brazil), 81
World Social Forum, 82

Zapatistas, 41
Žižek, Slavoj, 87n. 24, 90n. 64

◇

About the Author

Henry A. Giroux holds the Global TV Network Chair in Communications at McMaster University in Canada. His most recent books include: *Border Crossings* (Routledge, 2005); *Schooling and the Struggle for Public Life* (Paradigm, 2005); *Take Back Higher Education: Race, Youth, and the Crisis of Democracy in the Post Civil Rights Era* (Palgrave Macmillan, 2004); *The Terror of Neoliberalism* (Paradigm, 2004); and *The Abandoned Generation: Democracy Beyond the Culture of Fear* (Palgrave 2003), co-authored with Susan Searls Giroux. His primary research areas are cultural studies, youth studies, critical pedagogy, popular culture, media studies, social theory, and the politics of higher and public education.